AFRICA'S DISPLACED PEOPLE

HEARING

BEFORE THE

SUBCOMMITTEE ON AFRICA, GLOBAL HEALTH, GLOBAL HUMAN RIGHTS, AND INTERNATIONAL ORGANIZATIONS

OF THE

COMMITTEE ON FOREIGN AFFAIRS HOUSE OF REPRESENTATIVES

ONE HUNDRED FOURTEENTH CONGRESS

FIRST SESSION

JULY 9, 2015

Serial No. 114–86

Printed for the use of the Committee on Foreign Affairs

Available via the World Wide Web: http://www.foreignaffairs.house.gov/ or
http://www.gpo.gov/fdsys/

U.S. GOVERNMENT PUBLISHING OFFICE

95–424PDF · · · · WASHINGTON : 2015

For sale by the Superintendent of Documents, U.S. Government Publishing Office
Internet: bookstore.gpo.gov   Phone: toll free (866) 512–1800; DC area (202) 512–1800
Fax: (202) 512–2104   Mail: Stop IDCC, Washington, DC 20402–0001

COMMITTEE ON FOREIGN AFFAIRS

EDWARD R. ROYCE, California, *Chairman*

CHRISTOPHER H. SMITH, New Jersey
ILEANA ROS-LEHTINEN, Florida
DANA ROHRABACHER, California
STEVE CHABOT, Ohio
JOE WILSON, South Carolina
MICHAEL T. McCAUL, Texas
TED POE, Texas
MATT SALMON, Arizona
DARRELL E. ISSA, California
TOM MARINO, Pennsylvania
JEFF DUNCAN, South Carolina
MO BROOKS, Alabama
PAUL COOK, California
RANDY K. WEBER SR., Texas
SCOTT PERRY, Pennsylvania
RON DeSANTIS, Florida
MARK MEADOWS, North Carolina
TED S. YOHO, Florida
CURT CLAWSON, Florida
SCOTT DesJARLAIS, Tennessee
REID J. RIBBLE, Wisconsin
DAVID A. TROTT, Michigan
LEE M. ZELDIN, New York
DANIEL DONOVAN, New York

ELIOT L. ENGEL, New York
BRAD SHERMAN, California
GREGORY W. MEEKS, New York
ALBIO SIRES, New Jersey
GERALD E. CONNOLLY, Virginia
THEODORE E. DEUTCH, Florida
BRIAN HIGGINS, New York
KAREN BASS, California
WILLIAM KEATING, Massachusetts
DAVID CICILLINE, Rhode Island
ALAN GRAYSON, Florida
AMI BERA, California
ALAN S. LOWENTHAL, California
GRACE MENG, New York
LOIS FRANKEL, Florida
TULSI GABBARD, Hawaii
JOAQUIN CASTRO, Texas
ROBIN L. KELLY, Illinois
BRENDAN F. BOYLE, Pennsylvania

AMY PORTER, *Chief of Staff*   THOMAS SHEEHY, *Staff Director*
JASON STEINBAUM, *Democratic Staff Director* ₎

SUBCOMMITTEE ON AFRICA, GLOBAL HEALTH, GLOBAL HUMAN RIGHTS, AND INTERNATIONAL ORGANIZATIONS

CHRISTOPHER H. SMITH, New Jersey, *Chairman*

MARK MEADOWS, North Carolina
CURT CLAWSON, Florida
SCOTT DesJARLAIS, Tennessee
DANIEL DONOVAN, New York

KAREN BASS, California
DAVID CICILLINE, Rhode Island
AMI BERA, California

(II)

CONTENTS

WITNESSES

LETTERS, STATEMENTS, ETC., SUBMITTED FOR THE HEARING

APPENDIX

AFRICA'S DISPLACED PEOPLE

THURSDAY, JULY 9, 2015

House of Representatives,
Subcommittee on Africa, Global Health,
Global Human Rights, and International Organizations,
Committee on Foreign Affairs,
Washington, DC.

The subcommittee met, pursuant to notice, at 2:08 p.m., in room 2200, Rayburn House Office Building, Hon. Christopher H. Smith (chairman of the subcommittee) presiding.

Mr. SMITH. The hearing will come to order, and good afternoon, everybody. Sorry we are starting a few minutes late. Without objection, I am going to put my full statement in the record, and in conversations with our ranking member, she will likely make a statement shorter than we normally give, both of us, because there are a whole series of votes likely to be happening, and it is important to get to our witnesses.

Last year, nearly 60 million people were displaced worldwide. In fact, one out of every 122 people on Earth today is yet either a refugee, internally displaced in their home country, or seeking asylum in another country. In sub-Saharan Africa, there are more than 15 million displaced people. Of that total, 3.7 million are refugees, and 11.4 million are IDPs. These disruptions of normal life in Africa are caused by conflicts such as in Somalia, the Central African Republic, South Sudan, Nigeria, the Democratic Republic of the Congo, Mali, Burundi, Western Sahara, and elsewhere. These disruptions not only affect those who are displaced, but also the people in whose communities these displaced people are relocated.

African refugees and internally displaced people face numerous issues from security in the places in which they seek refuge, to death and mayhem trying to reach places of refuge, to conflict with surrounding populations to warehousing that consigns a generation to be born and live in foreign countries.

Today's hearing will exam the various issues displaced people face, and the U.S. response to these conditions in order to determine the effectiveness of our Government's efforts to help and to determine whether course corrections are necessary. The terrible plight of African refugees has been much in the news in recent months because of the deaths of thousands trying to reach Europe across the Mediterranean and attacks on refugees in South Africa reportedly caused by xenophobia.

So I, without objection, will put my full statement in the record. I yield to Mr. Cicilline for his opening.

(1)

Mr. CICILLINE. Thank you, Mr. Chairman, and thank you to you and our Ranking Member Bass for calling this important hearing today. And thank you to the witnesses for the testimony that you will provide.

The level of conflict and displacement around the world today is astounding, and the shocking number of 15 million people displaced in Africa is heartbreaking. Some of the conflicts that have upended people in Africa such as in Darfur, the DRC, and Somalia have gone on for decades, and we now face entire generations of children and their parents who have been born and raised away from their homelands. Many of these displaced persons have never lived outside of an IDP or refugee camp. They lack access to basic necessities and have little schooling.

Aside from the obvious tolls those conflicts have, they also have a lasting impact on generations of Africans. The United States is one of the largest donors to the U.N.'s High Commissioner for Refugees, as well as provides millions of dollars every year in bilateral humanitarian assistance, but needs still outpace global donations. So I look forward to hearing from our witnesses what more we can do to make certain that the needs of IDPs and refugees are being met, and thank you again for the testimony you are about to provide, and I yield back, Mr. Chairman.

Mr. SMITH. Thank you.

I would like to introduce our first two panelists, and I thank them for taking the time to be here and for their work and their dedication.

Beginning first with Ms. Catherine Wiesner, who is Deputy Assistant Secretary in the State Department's Bureau of Population, Refugees, and Migration, a position she has held since February 2012. She oversees the Offices of Assistance Programs for Africa, Multilateral Coordination and External Relations, and International Migration. She has also served as Principal Director to the Deputy Assistant Secretary of Defense for African Affairs in the Department of Defense. Previously she worked for UNICEF, the International Rescue Committee, UNHCR, and Save the Children.

Then we will hear from Mr. Thomas Staal, who is currently the Acting Assistant Administrator for the Bureau for Democracy, Conflict, and Humanitarian Assistance at USAID. He has worked for USAID since 1988, beginning in Sudan as an emergency program officer. He worked in the USAID regional office in Kenya managing food aid and project development throughout eastern and southern Africa. More recently, he served as the USAID Mission Director in Ethiopia. Before joining USAID, Mr. Staal worked for World Vision as their country representative in Sudan.

Catherine, if you could begin.

STATEMENT OF MS. CATHERINE WIESNER, DEPUTY ASSISTANT SECRETARY OF STATE, BUREAU OF POPULATION, REFUGEES, AND MIGRATION, U.S. DEPARTMENT OF STATE

Ms. WIESNER. Thank you, Chairman Smith, Ranking Member Bass, and members of the subcommittee for the opportunity to describe today what the State Department's Bureau of Population, Refugees, and Migration is doing in Africa to protect and assist African refugees and other persons of concern on the continent.

We should note that today is South Sudan's Independence Day, and it is a painful reminder of how conflict can undo progress and shatter hope. Instead of celebrating, South Sudan is embroiled in a humanitarian crisis that is the worst in Africa and one of the worst in the world.

In a year that set new records for displacement, Africa has not been spared. Today, we count 4½ million sub-Saharan refugees, and more than 11 million internally displaced. Burundi is the newest emergency. Some 150,000 refugees have already fled, fearing that political violence and intimidation could escalate into mass atrocities.

Mr. Chairman, as you noted, conflict continues to stalk Nigeria, South Sudan, the Central African Republic, Mali, Sudan, the Democratic Republic of the Congo, Somalia, and Libya, and for each country afflicted, there are two, three, four neighboring countries struggling to stop the violence from seeping across their borders and to host thousands and thousands of refugees. The vast majority of refugees flee to areas that are underdeveloped, remote, and difficult to reach. Moving civilians out of harm's way and providing life-saving assistance is expensive and it can be dangerous. Refugees often join vulnerable migrants on the move, lured by predatory smugglers taking advantage of lawlessness in Libya and elsewhere.

The humanitarian organizations that we support are stretched incredibly thin, but they are doing heroic work, standing up for humanitarian principles and finding creative ways to get around obstacles and to save lives.

U.S. leadership and our diplomatic and our financial support for these organizations are vital. Humanitarians are innovating and using new technology, such as biometric registration, cash transfers, and remote e-learning to improve services. Our Safe from the Start initiative is keeping more women and girls safe from gender-based violence.

On recent trips to Africa, I have seen the scale of the crisis we face, and I have also seen the importance of the aid that we provide. I was in Ethiopia a few months ago, which hosts more refugees than any other African nation. Refugees come from Eritrea, Sudan, South Sudan, and Somalia, and are found in camps on nearly every one of Ethiopia's borders, as well as in all its major cities and towns.

Many refugees set off for Europe and the Gulf states, despite the efforts of the government and humanitarian agencies. They know human smugglers may abuse them, kidnap them for ransom, or abandon them to die in the desert or drown at sea. It doesn't stop them because they would rather risk death than stay behind in places where they have no hope for any kind of future.

I just returned from Niger, one of the most impoverished countries in the world. Boko Haram's rampages have chased more than 100,000 people across the border from Nigeria, and displaced an additional 50,000 inside Niger. Many are scattered in villages where food is already scarce and insecurity restricts access. But agencies are responding creatively with cash transfers and vouchers and assisting all those in need based on vulnerability.

For pastoralist refugees from Mali, the Niger Government has set aside an extensive zone where they can move with their animals, allowing for greater self-sufficiency, and also dignity. In Niger and elsewhere, investments made in schools, clinics, and clean water for refugees and host communities alike contributes to local development while fostering peaceful coexistence.

We work closely with USAID and our diplomatic colleagues to resolve conflict. In the meantime, aiming to ensure that there is a safe place of refugee and that aid reaches internationally-accepted minimum standards. We and USAID are also working to develop greater coherence between relief and development assistance, particularly for protracted crises. Durable solutions can seem elusive. Al-Shabaab's atrocities have set Kenya on edge, and while U.S. diplomacy has worked to prevent Somalis from being forced back prematurely, they still get branded wrongfully as potential terrorists.

Darfuris in Chad still need protection and struggle to achieve self-reliance. Political stalemate on the Western Sahara has left Sahrawis languishing for far too long in Algeria. And the Ebola epi- demic has delayed efforts to bring Ivoirian refugees home from Li- beria. And yet there are bright spots: Tanzania and Zambia are allowing more refugees to stay permanently, and some to become citizens. Some 19,000 African refugees will find new homes in the United States through our resettlement program this year.

My Bureau expects to program nearly $800 million across the continent of Africa this fiscal year, channeling our funds through leading humanitarian organizations, such as the U.N. Refugee Agency, the International Committee of the Red Cross, the International Organization for Migration, and a range of other aid groups. Even with this record amount, we cannot claim to be meeting all of the needs, even at the most basic level. We can, thanks to the generosity of Congress, confidently say that we are saving many lives, and we are assisting millions to live in greater dignity and with hope for a better future.

Thank you, again, for holding this important hearing, and I look forward to any questions.

[The prepared statement of Ms. Wiesner follows:]

Testimony of U.S Department of State
Deputy Assistant Secretary Catherine Wiesner
Bureau for Population, Refugees and Migration

House Foreign Affairs Committee Subcommittee on Africa, Global Health, Global Human Rights, and International Organizations

"Africa's Displaced People"

July 9, 2015

Thank you Mr. Chairman, Ranking Member Bass, and Members of the Subcommittee for this opportunity to describe what the U.S. government, and in particular the State Department's Bureau of Population, Refugees, and Migration is doing to protect and assist African refugees and other persons of concern on the continent.

As you probably know given your interest in African affairs, today, July 9, happens to be South Sudan's independence day. It is a fitting day for this hearing, although unfortunately not in celebration of a long civil war resolved, but because South Sudan has rapidly gone from being the world's newest country full of hope to one of the most severe humanitarian crises in Africa today. There are now more new South Sudanese refugees – 592,700 – than there were when the Comprehensive Peace Agreement was signed 10 years ago.

On World Refugee Day last month the UN High Commissioner for Refugees released his annual Global Trends report showing that the number of uprooted people is at the highest levels ever recorded, and accelerating rapidly. What does this mean for Africa? At the end of 2014, sub-Saharan Africa had 3.7 million refugees and 11.4 million internally displaced persons, 4.5 million of whom were newly displaced over the course of the year. Burundi is the latest crisis in this troubling trend, where more than 150,000 new refugees have fled political violence and intimidation as fears grow that the mass atrocities we have worked hard over the last few years to prevent could still take place. Burundi is the newest emergency, but the list of countries in crisis in Africa remains long: Nigeria, South Sudan, the Central African Republic, Mali, Sudan, the Democratic Republic of Congo, Somalia, Libya. And for each of these countries embroiled in war or chronic instability, there are two, three, even four or more neighboring countries affected by streams of refugees; and sometimes the violence that caused them to flee seeps across borders as well.

Almost nine out of every ten refugees in the world are in countries – and regions of those countries – considered less economically developed. This is especially apparent in Africa and creates myriad challenges in even simply reaching refugees in remote areas with life-saving assistance and help to move out of harm's way. At the same time, more and more refugees are living in urban settings, requiring a new set of tools and strategies. Moreover, we have seen a substantial increase in out-migration from the continent, facilitated in significant part by lawlessness in Libya and a growing industry in human smuggling.

As an example of these phenomena, Ethiopia hosts refugees from nearly all of its neighbors -- Eritrea, Sudan, South Sudan, and Somalia. It replaced Kenya last year as the largest refugee-hosting country in Africa, and is the fifth largest worldwide. Ethiopia is also a significant origin and transit country for onward migration; refugees fleeing violence and persecution mix with economic migrants seeking a better future. They leave Ethiopia for Sudan, en route to Libya and eventually Europe, while others continue to cross into Djibouti en route to Yemen and Gulf States beyond. In the other direction, South Africa is another important destination. The tragedies that befall migrants from across Africa on these dangerous journeys are terrible and known – falling victim to traffickers and xenophobic violence, being kidnapped for ransom, even dying of dehydration in the desert or drowning at sea – but people continue to seek alternatives for themselves and their families despite the perils.

In terms of the M in PRM, we support governments to better manage migration through programs that build upon the expertise of the International Organization for Migration and UNHCR to enhance regional dialogues among States, build the capacity of government officials, and promote protection screening and assistance for the most vulnerable migrants. To complement these efforts, PRM launched an initiative with several other States last year called "Migrants in Countries in Crisis" to address situations like that of the Central African Republic, where people from many countries found themselves caught up in someone else's conflict.

The brutality of conflict, the growing gap between needs and resources, and the protracted nature of displacement in Africa all mean more human suffering; this is undeniable. The human and financial resources of the humanitarian organizations upon which we rely, including UNHCR, ICRC, IOM, and other international and non-governmental organizations, are stretched incredibly thin in responding to new emergencies on top of persistent crises. But I would stress that even in the most trying circumstances, the committed staff of these organizations continue their heroic work, standing up for humanitarian principles even in the face of flagrant disregard by warring parties, and consistently seeking new and creative ways to help. U.S. humanitarian leadership in supporting these organizations both financially and diplomatically is extraordinarily important.

The scale of need has pushed everyone in the humanitarian community to more urgently explore new ways of doing business, such as UNHCR's "alternative to camps" approach. We continue to support our partners to innovate and seek efficiencies in the delivery of humanitarian assistance – for example, the implementation of biometric registration and the use of vouchers and cash transfers. Partnerships with the private sector have helped connect students and teachers in remote refugee camps to the internet, making e-learning possible for the first time. At PRM we have maintained our long-standing focus on protection, especially of women and girls, from gender based violence. Under the joint State Department and USAID initiative, *"Safe from the Start"* we have invested resources in the institutional changes – policies, staffing, training – necessary for our primary partners to ensure that the safety of women and girls is prioritized in every humanitarian response.

A few weeks ago I had the opportunity to visit Niger, which offers a rich picture of some of these displacement and migration challenges, as well as some of the innovative responses undertaken with U.S. support. One of the countries in Africa ranked lowest on the Human Development Index, Niger hosts refugees from both Nigeria and Mali. It is also an historic crossroads for primarily economic migration from West Africa northward. IOM predicts that 100,000 migrants will transit through the northern desert town of Agadez this year on their way to Libya and Europe, and has warned of growing signs of trafficking of young women and girls within the overall smuggling of migrants.

Boko Haram violence has forced more than 100,000 Nigerian refugees plus Nigerien migrants who had long lived in Nigeria to seek safety in Niger. Attacks by Boko Haram inside Niger have resulted in an additional 50,000 Nigerien internally displaced persons. Most refugees, returnees, and internally displaced persons are living dispersed across numerous villages with Nigerien hosts who are themselves impoverished and facing food insecurity. Humanitarian access has been restricted by insecurity and ongoing military operations. But agencies are endeavoring to work within these constraints, employing creative responses such as mobile protection monitors, and cash transfers and vouchers in lieu of direct distribution of food and other household supplies. While UNHCR has set up two camps for refugees and IDPs, transfer to the camps is voluntary. Aid is also provided outside of camps for all those in need, based on vulnerability. This model agreed among aid agencies and with the government is a sensible approach that should be replicated elsewhere in mixed settings.

For those Malian refugees with a traditional pastoralist lifestyle, Niger has also adopted an alternative to camps, setting aside an extensive area where they can move with their animals. The "zone" model has been very successful in promoting relative self-sufficiency and independence for refugees. Investments by the international community in additional water points, a clinic, and a school that has become the largest in the region have benefited both the local population and the refugee community, contributing simultaneously to local development and peaceful co-existence.

While this general strategy to include host populations in some of the basic assistance provided to refugees has been in place for quite a while, we do see that in some of the more protracted situations, fatigue in hosting refugees has nonetheless set in. The situation of Somali refugees in Kenya is perhaps one of the most dramatic examples, and a place where we have invested considerable diplomatic effort to preserve their ability to maintain asylum there despite some claims that refugees are connected to domestic terrorism threats. A pilot voluntary return program to several areas in Somalia is underway, but conditions are not yet ripe for large-scale returns.

Every protracted refugee situation has unique characteristics. Darfuris in Chad and Sahrawis in Algeria are two additional long-staying populations for which UNHCR faces context-specific obstacles to finding solutions. In Chad self-sufficiency efforts are constrained by the dearth of development actors, while continued insecurity prevents the voluntary return of refugees to Darfur. In Tindouf, Sahrawis remain victims of a political stalemate where open conflict is in hiatus but the international community has not addressed the root causes. Both refugee communities are situated in harsh desert environments, frustrating efforts to at least promote greater self-reliance. Another refugee situation that should be resolved, but has been repeatedly delayed, is the voluntary return of Ivoirian refugees from Liberia, initially put on hold by the Ivoirian government because of fears of the spread of Ebola.

While examples of durable solutions for refugees and internally displaced persons can seem few and far between, there are bright spots of which we should not lose sight. Both Tanzania and Zambia have in the last few years made significant progress pursuing pragmatic durable solutions, offering pathways to local integration through permanent residency and in some cases naturalization for refugees who have now lived in their countries for generations. UNHCR is pursuing renewed and strengthened partnerships with development agencies and other development actors to promote interim and sustainable solutions. Following a recent World Bank-UNHCR joint study on the development effects of refugees, returned refugees, and IDPs in the Great Lakes region of Africa, the governments of Tanzania, Zambia, and the Democratic Republic of the Congo have approved loans for longer-term projects benefiting displaced persons and hosting communities in their countries.

While only 126,800 refugees returned to their country of origin with UNHCR assistance last year – the lowest number recorded since 1983 – the majority of these voluntary returns were in Africa (Democratic Republic of the Congo, Mali, Angola, Sudan, Côte d'Ivoire and Rwanda). And despite the low overall numbers, the opportunity to finally return home is obviously of great significance to those individuals and families able to do so.

Furthermore, the U.S. Refugee Admissions Program is resettling African refugees of at least 29 nationalities, providing an important durable solution to some of the most vulnerable refugees without other alternatives. As part of this program, a major effort is underway to resettle longtime Congolese refugees to the United States. The U.S. will admit some 19,000 refugees from Africa in FY2015.

In all of these situations – whether new or protracted – we work closely with our USAID colleagues on humanitarian assistance. We work closely with our diplomatic colleagues to push for an end to the persecution and conflict that produce displacement across the continent. While the search for political solutions continues, we aim to ensure that there is a safe place of refuge and that basic material aid reaches internationally-accepted minimum standards. We are working with our USAID colleagues as well to develop greater coherence between relief and development assistance, particularly for protracted crises. Last year, the U.S. government provided nearly $2.5 billion in humanitarian assistance in Africa -- of which PRM obligated more than $780 million. Given the rise in needs, PRM expects to program nearly $800 million across the continent of Africa in FY 2015. Even with this record amount, we cannot claim to be meeting all of the needs, even at the most basic level. But thanks to the generosity of Congress, we can confidently say that we are saving many lives and assisting millions of people to live in greater dignity and with more hope for a better future.

Thank you again for holding this important hearing. I would be happy to answer questions you may have.

Mr. SMITH. Ms. Wiesner, thank you very much for your testimony.

Mr. Staal.

STATEMENT OF MR. THOMAS H. STAAL, ACTING ASSISTANT ADMINISTRATOR, BUREAU FOR DEMOCRACY, CONFLICT, AND HUMANITARIAN ASSISTANCE, U.S. AGENCY FOR INTERNATIONAL DEVELOPMENT

Mr. STAAL. Chairman Smith, Ranking Member Bass, and members of the subcommittee, thank you for inviting me to testify today, and for your continuing support for USAID's assistance to the displaced throughout Africa.

As my colleague Catherine has just mentioned, we are grappling today with the largest global displacement in recorded history. Whereas in the past, natural disasters triggered mass movements of people across Africa, terrorism and ethnic and sectarian strife are now increasingly driving record numbers of people from their homes. Across Africa, the most vulnerable are the hardest hit—in the midst of power grabs by armed forces, governments, and terrorists. Women are facing new levels of terror, rape, and forced indoctrination. Children have been stripped of their innocence and inflicted untold tortures by armed groups.

But amidst these horrors, there are countless affected individuals in search of peace: The girls from Chibok, Nigeria, lucky enough to escape the grips of Boko Haram, Imam Omar; Archbishop Dieudonne and Reverend Guerekoyame, from the Central African Republic, who are bringing communities together to heal the scars of war and find faith in the power of forgiveness; the children of Bor in South Sudan who continue to learn in their native Dinka through our mobile literacy programs. Their courage and resilience in the face of brutality reminds us why we must continue and to do more to help.

Despite resource, access, and security constraints, we are doing everything possible to reach Africa's displaced people with life-saving assistance. For instance, in South Sudan, we are the largest humanitarian donor. Since the current crisis began in December 2013, we have provided $1.2 billion in food, shelter, clean water, health care, and psychological support to the people. As fighting rages on, more than 40 percent of the country now faces life-threatening hunger. Our humanitarian aid is an essential lifeline for those who are suffering from this senseless violence.

In Nigeria, we are making sure displaced and host communities have access to health care, vaccines and clean water. We are also supporting informal education centers for displaced children. And thanks to the flexibilities provided to—in our food aid accounts, we have provided food vouchers to over 100,000 Nigerians in conflict. And with these vouchers, they can buy healthy foods in the local market, which helps to combat malnutrition and restart economic activity in these war-ravaged areas.

We are also committed to protecting women, children, and other vulnerable groups. For instance, we are providing health and psychosocial support to victims of gender-based violence in South Sudan, and to survivors of Boko Haram's abuses in Nigeria. In the Central African Republic (CAR), we worked with UNICEF to negotiate the release of 3,300 boys and girls from armed groups and re-integrate them back with their families.

We know that the plight of displaced people will not lessen unless we address the root causes of violence and state fragility at the heart of Africa's displacement crisis. That is why we are investing in peace building, promoting inclusive governance, and expanding educational and economic opportunities for Africa's most marginalized communities. Our Office of Transition Initiatives is addressing the conditions that have allowed extremists like Boko Haram to flourish.

Through innovative sports and radio programs, we are working with local communities, especially young people, to overcome feelings of exclusion and the lure of extremism. We have harnessed conflict early warning tools and engaged in concerted diplomacy through the interagency Atrocity Prevention Board to address flashpoints of instability.

In CAR, the Complex Crisis Fund, and other programs have proven critical in preventing genocide and mass atrocities, expanding the space to safely provide humanitarian assistance, facilitating the conditions for peaceful transition. USAID has provided $7.5 million to promote community dialogue, especially between groups of different faiths in CAR, and we are reviving local media networks to provide accurate information and dispel rumors that are spreading fear. And we have launched the CAR Peace Partnership, which is providing several million in private donations linked with $7 million of USAID funding to support CAR's transition over the next 5 years.

We may not have stopped the violence in CAR, but we have been able to improve security conditions, allowing people to begin to return home, laying groundwork for peace. These efforts, and many more, are helping Africa's displaced to rebuild their lives, restore tolerance in their communities, and realize their aspirations for a more peaceful and prosperous future.

We thank the subcommittee and its members for their long-standing support, which makes these efforts possible. Thank you very much, and I look forward to your questions.

[The prepared statement of Mr. Staal follows:]

Testimony of U.S. Agency for International Development
Acting Assistant Administrator Thomas H. Staal
Bureau for Democracy, Conflict, and Humanitarian Assistance

House Foreign Affairs Committee Subcommittee on Africa, Global Health, Global Human Rights, and International Organizations

"Africa's Displaced People"

July 9, 2015

Chairman Smith, Ranking Member Bass, and Members of the Subcommittee, thank you for inviting me to testify on USAID's assistance to displaced populations in Africa. Thank you also for your support for USAID's humanitarian and development programs around the globe. Thanks to your assistance, we are not only saving lives, but restoring a sense of dignity and hope for millions of displaced families striving to reknit the fabric of their lives after bearing witness to untold horrors.

Introduction

Today, we are grappling with the largest global displacement in recorded history. Nearly 60 million people have been uprooted from their homes, fleeing across borders as refugees or within their own countries to escape rampant violence, persecution, and destruction. More than half of all refugees are children, too many of whom have had their innocence stripped away after suffering abuse, seeing parents or relatives killed, or leaving their homes in the chaotic fog of war.

More than a quarter of all of the world's displaced persons are in Africa. Conflict is now driving enormous numbers of people from their homes to seek refuge elsewhere. In Mali and Nigeria, governments are struggling to beat back the scourge of violent extremism, especially in communities where weak governance and lack of economic opportunities provide breeding grounds for radicalism. South Sudan is mired in a spiral of brutal violence and retribution that has left more than two million people displaced, hungry, and terrorized. Political unrest in Burundi has caused 150,000 people to flee to neighboring countries. Today's flashpoints are layered on top of decades-long instability in Somalia, Sudan, and the Democratic Republic of Congo (DRC) that continue to drive millions from their homes.

Behind these staggering figures and enormous challenges are the individuals in search of peace, such as the women and children—including girls from Chibok, Nigeria—who are lucky enough to escape the grips of Boko Haram and are trying to rebuild their lives, pursue an education, and overcome the chilling horrors of captivity, rape, and forced indoctrination. Imam Omar, Archbishop Dieudonné and Reverend Guerékoyame from the Central African Republic (CAR) are bringing communities of all religions together to heal the scars of war and find faith in the power of forgiveness. The children of Bor, South Sudan—continue to learn in their native tongue, Dinka Cham—through USAID's *All Children Reading* mobile literacy program. Their resilience in the face of brutality reminds us why we must do more to help Africa's displaced people regain a sense of normalcy and prospects for a better future. We are compelled to help not only out of a sense of humanity but also as a national security priority to foster stability and peace in the world's youngest continent.

Today, I would like to share what USAID is doing to save lives and alleviate the suffering of Africa's displaced communities, including the most vulnerable among them—such as women, children, the elderly, and the disabled. I will focus on our efforts in three countries—South Sudan, CAR and Nigeria—where the needs are particularly acute and USAID has invested significant resources. I would also like to highlight our efforts to address the root causes of conflict, which is driving record-level displacement.

Humanitarian response

Over the past five years, violent events, including terrorism and civil unrest, have exploded across Africa. Protracted conflicts in South Sudan, Nigeria, DRC, and CAR—coupled with complex crises in the Middle East—are straining the humanitarian system like never before. In 2014, USAID's Office of U.S. Foreign Disaster Assistance (OFDA) and the Office of Food for Peace (FFP) responded to four Level Three—the United Nation's most severe emergency designation—humanitarian crises, including in South Sudan and CAR, as well as West Africa's Ebola outbreak. Our contributions to addressing global crises, as well as those of other donors, however, are outpaced by the rate at which needs are growing. As violence across the continent shows no signs of abating, many Africans have been uprooted more than once and will likely be unable to return home for years, if not decades. According to the United Nations High Commissioner for Refugees (UNHCR), the average duration of forced displacement is 17 years.

The sheer scale and protracted nature of displacement, and growing demands on stretched humanitarian budgets, present special challenges for meeting the needs of Africa's displaced. Often, we struggle to gain access to those most in need, whether they are dispersed in remote areas cut off from reliable transportation routes, or among host communities generous enough to take them in. Our humanitarian partners are increasingly operating in dangerous environments, and attacks against them are increasing accordingly. In the past decade, the number of aid workers reportedly killed, wounded, or kidnapped globally has almost doubled; there were 335 major security incidents last year.

In South Sudan, several of our partner staff have gone missing. The South Sudanese government recently expelled the United Nations (UN) top humanitarian official Toby Lanzer for speaking out against the senseless violence and rampant impunity that has left the country one of the most food insecure places in the world. Increased violence has closed off essential routes for aid delivery by the UN World Food Programme (WFP) and other partners. To stave off famine, we have had to resort to delivering aid through air operations, which are significantly more expensive than delivering aid by trucks. In another example, in Boko Haram-affected areas of Northeast Nigeria, the presence of trained, capable humanitarian workers has expanded but is still limited.

Despite these challenges, we are doing everything possible to reach Africa's displaced communities with life-saving assistance. Our efforts primarily focus on providing relief for internally displaced persons (IDPs), those who flee their homes due to conflict, human rights abuses, or natural disasters but who have not crossed an international border. We do this in concert with the Department of State's Bureau of Population, Refugees, and Migration, which targets the needs of refugees.

In Fiscal Year 2014, USAID provided more than $481 million in humanitarian assistance to Africa, helping tens of millions of IDPs. We leveraged flexible tools such as Rapid Response Funds—which provide quick routing of funding to partners in emergency situations—to mobilize timely responses to newly displaced populations in South Sudan and elsewhere. We delivered emergency health services to IDPs across Africa to combat the spread of disease in conflict zones where healthcare systems have been decimated. We provided support to shared UN services that facilitate larger international relief efforts, including the UN Humanitarian Air Service to support humanitarian staff movements, the UN Department of Safety and Security to conduct security assessments, and the International Organization for Migration (IOM) to track population movements.

We also delivered approximately $1.2 billion in emergency food assistance across the continent, including to millions of both internally displaced people and refugees. Thanks to reforms in the Farm Bill that increased the amount of cash available under Title II food aid programs, we were able to reach an additional 600,000 people with food assistance in Africa and worldwide in 2014. These flexibilities, along with our Emergency Food Security Program (EFSP) funded through the International Disaster Assistance (IDA) account, meant that we were able to use a mix of U.S. in-kind, regionally purchased, and cash-based food assistance to meet growing demands for food aid across Africa. These flexibilities and the additional 25 percent increased flexibility in Title II funds requested by President Obama in the 2015 and 2016 budgets are essential to ensuring we can respond swiftly, effectively, and efficiently to combat hunger in Africa in a time of complex crises around the world.

Nigeria, which faces numerous conflicts within its borders in addition to the Boko Haram insurgency, has nearly 1.8 million people displaced either internally or to neighboring countries. We have provided nearly $56 million in humanitarian assistance to help those in the region affected by the conflict and more than $1.4 billion in other foreign assistance over the past two fiscal years. In Northeast Nigeria—where Boko Haram has spread a brutal brand of terror, sadism and destruction—we are supporting humanitarian, transitional, and development efforts in collaboration with the Government of Nigeria at both the federal and local level. We provide displaced and host communities with health and vaccination services, water and sanitation, food assistance, and support to informal education centers for IDP children.

Our Office of Food for Peace, which is the lead office providing food assistance to both refugees and IDPs around the world, is providing cash transfers and food vouchers to over 100,000 displaced persons and host communities in Yobe, Gombe, and Adamawa states of Nigeria, targeting pregnant and lactating women, female-headed households, and households with children under five. This cash-based assistance allows people to buy nutritious foods in local markets, thereby helping to combat malnutrition and restart economic activity in areas ravaged by Boko Haram. Through voucher-for-work programs, we are also trying to empower displaced and host families that have had their livelihoods disrupted by violence and instability. We also launched village savings and loan groups and trained farmers in herd management, animal health, and livestock feed conservation so that they can rebuild their assets and get back to farming.

As Boko Haram expands its reach into neighboring Cameroon, we have responded adeptly to help those in need. For instance, our partner IOM used its Displacement Tracking Matrix —a database that tracks population movements—to target and provide relief items to more than 2,000 people in Cameroon's Far North Region, where both Cameroonian IDPs and Nigerian refugees have fled Boko Haram incursions over the past year.

In South Sudan, the U.S. government has long been the largest donor, providing $1.2 billion in emergency assistance to conflict-affected and displaced populations since the start of the crisis in 2013. These efforts have provided much-needed food, shelter, clean water, health care, and psychological support for the people of South Sudan. Last month, we announced an additional $115 million in humanitarian assistance, and this fiscal year alone we have provided more than 138,000 tons of U.S. and regionally procured food. Nevertheless, as fighting rages on, many are stuck in overcrowded peacekeeping bases that were meant as temporary housing for those who initially fled when the conflict erupted in December 2013. Children are not able to go to school, families have been torn apart, and farmers cannot harvest crops. Up to 4.6 million people—40 percent of the population—face life-threatening hunger this month. As a result of the conflict, USAID has redirected its development assistance, shifting from state-building to more directly assisting the people of South Sudan.

In the midst of competing priorities and strained resources, we have not lost, and cannot lose, sight of CAR, where more than one in five of its 4.6 million inhabitants is displaced. Acute violence has compromised CAR's decades-long peaceful coexistence between Muslims and Christians and devastated a country that was already languishing under the weight of neglect, woefully weak governance, and some of the lowest development indicators on Earth. USAID has provided more than $142 million in humanitarian relief and food assistance to the people of CAR in the past two fiscal years. Our efforts are focused on providing fast and flexible assistance for the displaced, as well as those seeking to return home. In a country with tough terrain and sporadic bouts of violence that complicate access, we also reinforced the humanitarian coordination and information sharing, funded transportation to hard-to-reach areas through the UN Humanitarian Air Service, and supported security analyses to help facilitate relief operations in insecure areas.

We provide a mix of in-kind food, including Ready–to–Use Therapeutic Foods (RUTF) for children with severe acute malnutrition, as well as locally and regionally purchased food and cash–based food vouchers, to IDPs in CAR and refugees from CAR in Cameroon, Chad, DRC, and the Republic of Congo (RoC). We are also providing employment opportunities, cash vouchers, as well as seeds, tools and basic agricultural training so that the people of CAR can get back on their feet.

We have seen an uptick in people returning home in CAR. Returnees like Odette Kofedanga are determined to persevere against all odds. Odette fled her village in western CAR when it was attacked by armed rebels in 2013. Her friends and neighbors were killed, 550 homes were burned and all means of earning an income were vandalized or taken away. Odette hid in the bush with her eight children for months, where she says they was forced to "live like animals," eating wild plants to survive. Her children went without food for days at a time. When security improved, she went back her village and enrolled in a USAID-funded WFP program in which families received food rations, as well as seeds, tools, and fertilizer to start farming again. The food ration helped Odette feed her family and avoid selling off or eating the seeds she received, so that she could plant the next harvest. She was able to grow corn and sell it to buy clothes and enroll her children back in school. Each day, there are more "Odettes" in CAR, planting the seeds for a better tomorrow.

Protecting women and children
There is a Swahili saying that says, "When two elephants fight, it is the grass that gets trampled." Across Africa, the most vulnerable communities are worst hit by violence, forced to flee in the midst of power grabs by armed forces, governments, extremists, and others who seek to impose their will by force. And we know that women, children, and the elderly often bear the heaviest burden. At USAID, we are committed to protecting women, children, and other vulnerable groups in crisis situations as part of the U.S. government's Safe from the Start Initiative and its Action Plan on Children in Adversity. To date in FY 2015, USAID has provided nearly $40 million in humanitarian protection activities to meet these commitments in Africa.

According to a UN report released last week, a government-led campaign in South Sudan has ratcheted up violence and acts of torture, especially against women and children, to a new level of brutality and intensity. In at least nine separate incidents, South Sudan's army gang raped and burned women and children alive in their homes. A UNICEF report out this month documents horrific crimes against children, including castration, rape, and killings. We are appalled by these unconscionable acts committed by all parties to the conflict, and continue to stand with the South Sudanese people by providing aid to all those in need regardless of ethnicity.

Since the crisis began in South Sudan we have prioritized efforts to combat rampant Gender-Based Violence (GBV). We are we are providing psychosocial services for those who are displaced at the largest IDP site in the country—the base of the UN Mission in South Sudan (UNMISS) in Bentiu—and through programs that educate women on the dangers of GBV and provide critical and life-saving health and emotional support for GBV survivors. As the majority of displaced people are sheltering in rural areas outside of UN bases, we also provide clinical and psychosocial support and treatment services to children and women survivors there.

There is perhaps no greater crime than committing atrocities against children. Yet too many children have been stripped of their innocence and suffered untold horrors inflicted by armed groups in South Sudan, CAR, Nigeria, and other conflict-zones across Africa. According to UNICEF, Africa has the greatest number—and highest rate of increase—of conscripted children in the world. There are approximately 20,000 children associated with armed conflict in CAR and South Sudan alone. Wide-scale displacement has also left many children separated from their families and caretakers. USAID provides critical assistance to help African displaced children shed the trauma of conflict. In South Sudan, we are working with a local non-governmental organization (NGO), Street Children Aid, to provide safe spaces for both host community and displaced children to learn and protect them from the risk of sexual exploitation or recruitment into armed groups. In CAR, where our partner UNICEF has negotiated the release of 3,300 boys and girls from armed groups over the past two years, we support the delivery of life-saving assistance to these children, as well as healthcare, psychosocial support, and family reintegration assistance. We also provide older children with vocational training so that they can get jobs and avoid re-recruitment into armed activity.

In northeastern Nigeria, Boko Haram continues to abduct young women, girls, and boys, forcing them through rape and terror into adopting its nihilist ideology. We are coordinating with the Government of Nigeria to provide psychosocial support to survivors of Boko Haram violence. Through a $4.5 million, five-year (2010-15) program, we are supporting psychosocial support activities, such as counseling to survivors of Boko Haram's abuses and their families, including those directly affected by the abduction in Chibok. We and the U.S. embassy team in Abuja are also working with the Government of Nigeria to ensure that the safety, well-being, and dignity of Boko Haram survivors are prioritized during their reintegration back to their families and communities.

In addition to these stand-alone protection activities, our Office of U.S. Foreign Disaster Assistance carefully reviews all humanitarian programs to ensure that proposed activities do not create unintended dangers or cause harm for vulnerable populations, including sexual exploitation of women and children. For example, we require that grantees consult communities on how to organize distribution lines, taking into account location and ease of access, so that women and girls do not have to travel too far or at night to receive aid.

Addressing the root causes of displacement
We know that the plight of the displaced will not improve unless the root causes of violence and state fragility are addressed. At USAID, contingency funds, including our Transition Initiative Account and Complex Crisis Fund, are important resources that allow us to design sophisticated, locally-informed responses to address the root causes of complex crises. However, the growing magnitude of these types of crises around the world means that the current levels of these resources are not adequate to meet the needs.

Promoting Inclusive Governance
At the heart of Africa's simmering conflicts are unstable relationships between societies and their states. That is why USAID prioritizes democracy, human rights, and governance as a cornerstone of our development agenda. Throughout Africa, we promote inclusive political participation, so that people can speak without fear, have a say in the policies of their governments, and see their aspirations realized and facilitated through good governance, rule of law, and broad-based economic growth and opportunity.

For instance, in northern Nigeria, our Leadership, Empowerment, Advocacy and Development (LEAD) program is building partnerships between state and local governments, civil society, and the private sector to improve governance, accountability, and the delivery of essential services to citizens in Bauchi and Sokoto states.

The Nigeria Regional Transition Initiative led by USAID's Office of Transition Initiatives is designed to address the conditions that have allowed extremist groups such as Boko Haram to flourish in northeastern Nigeria. Through small, strategic assistance to local groups, we are improving government responsiveness to citizen expectations, reducing perceptions of marginalization and exploring efforts to reduce youth vulnerability to extremism influences. We are bringing young Nigerians together in sport-for-peace events that reinforce the value of sportsmanship and comradery. We have also launched the first-ever shortwave broadcast in Kanuri, the primary language spoken in northeastern Nigeria and border areas most affected by Boko Haram. It features stories of daily life and conveys to this traditionally marginalized community that others are paying attention to their crisis. One fan recently wrote the following message to the producers: "We thank you for giving us a place to air our voice and listen in our dialect." Without a doubt, these efforts are making an invaluable difference in the lives of communities that have been displaced, terrorized, and alienated, offering the familiar comfort of a voice in their native tongue. However, resource constraints have curtailed our ability to maintain or expand the geographic reach of these initiatives and others aimed at addressing the root causes that allow Boko Haram to exist.

In advance of Nigeria's historic election in April, USAID invested $51 million to work closely with Nigeria's election authorities, political parties, and civil society to promote peaceful political participation and a free, fair, and credible electoral process. Innovative campaigns, such as #VoteNotFight, mobilized youth through radio, social media, and importantly, grassroots campaigning, to have their voices heard and promote peaceful elections. These young campaigners should stand proud: thanks to their efforts, and those of many others, Nigeria has ushered in a historic and peaceful transfer of power, a hopeful harbinger for Africa's future.

Expanding Opportunity
Boko Haram means "Western education is unclean," underscoring the importance the group places on denying children the opportunity to expand their worldview. In areas overtaken by this criminal gang of extremists, schools have been bombed and children kidnapped and indoctrinated. Boko Haram specifically targets girls whom it believes have no right to an education. Even before Boko Haram emerged, the educational system in Northern Nigeria was underperforming compared to the rest of the country. A recent USAID-funded assessment of reading skills in the Northern Nigerian states of Bauchi and Sokoto found that 70 percent of third grade students could not read a single word of a simple narrative text.

In an effort to address deeply entrenched grievances, cultural differences, and under-investment in education in Nigeria's Northeast, USAID has launched several education efforts. A $20.5 million crisis response program is providing basic education to internally displaced persons and other conflict-affected communities through informal, community-managed schools. These efforts will be reinforced over the longer-term by our new flagship five-year, $120 million Northern Education Initiative Plus expands upon a previous effort to strengthen education systems so that they can provide greater access and improve reading among primary school children.

Fostering Peace and Reconciliation
We know that while bolstering the state's capacity to deliver to its citizens is critical to promoting peace in Africa, most displaced communities will not return home unless they are at peace with their neighbors. Throughout Africa, USAID seeks to target its humanitarian and development programs in ways that mitigate tensions and create bridges for shared peace and prosperity between communities.

Through the Complex Crisis Fund, concerted diplomacy and early warning response through the Atrocity Prevention Board and other efforts, we have not only been able to foster peace after the outbreak of conflict, but address flashpoints of instability before they spark. For instance, USAID's Complex Crises Fund and other programs in CAR aim to prevent genocide and mass atrocities, expand the space to safely provide humanitarian assistance, and support conditions favorable to a peaceful political transition. To that end, USAID has provided $7.5 million to empower local voices for peace, promote interreligious and other community dialogue, and help dispel rumors and fear mongering by improving access to accurate information from local media.

These are important first steps, but we recognize that dedicated long-term funding is necessary to truly transform societal relations in CAR. That is why we launched the CAR Peace Partnership last year, which will use up to $7 million of USAID funds to strengthen locally-led peacebuilding and atrocity prevention efforts in CAR for the next five years, laying a stronger foundation for the transitional processes underway in the country. USAID has received pledges for several million dollars of cash and in-kind support for this partnership from the private sector. Day by day, these efforts are fostering peace at the community level, and making it easier for returnees to rebuild their lives.

Conclusion
At USAID, we are committing to doing everything possible to save lives and alleviate suffering among Africa's displaced communities. At the root of Africa's displacement crisis are communities that lack the political and economic conditions to prosper peacefully. That is why we are also investing in bolstering good governance and expanding the space for opportunity in Africa's most marginalized communities. These efforts support USAID's enduring mission of ending extreme poverty and promoting resilient, democratic societies where people can live peacefully and without fear of being uprooted.

We thank the subcommittee and its Members for their longstanding support, which makes our efforts possible. I look forward to your questions.

Mr. SMITH. Thank you very much, Mr. Staal, for your leadership and for your testimony today.

Let me ask you if I could, especially since you did work with World Vision in the past, and both of you might want to speak to this. You know, Africa is a continent of faith, and from my travels, sometimes the faith community, for whatever reason, is not included as robustly as it should. I know you know that, and I am wondering if you could just tell us when it comes to IDPs and refugees, is there a plan, an aggressive effort to try to build on the economies of scale that would be provided?

To give an example, I was in Jos a few years ago with Greg Simpkins, and while we were there—it is a place where Boko Haram has slaughtered many people. We went to fire-bombed churches while we were there. We met with Archbishop Kaigama and also met with the Muslim leadership who worked very, very closely together. And then we went to an IDP camp that was grossly underfunded and in great need. The Jubilee Campaign was providing some funding, and, as a matter of fact, one of the men I met there who actually had a gun put to his head, an AK–47, and was told to renounce his faith in Christ, he said: No. I am ready to meet my Lord, and they blew his face off, and you could see the results of that. They left him for dead. We brought him here courtesy of the Jubilee Campaign. He testified in 2172. You could have heard a pin drop, you might recall, when he testified about what he had been through.

But at the IDP camp where I met him, it was with great regret that they were not getting the kind of help that they need. And, you know, I brought that to the attention of the Embassy. I hope that there has been an effort to try to reach out and do that. You did point out some of the numbers, and I know, you know, it is always, do you have the budget? Do you have the wherewithal? Is Congress providing enough? It is a shared responsibility.

So if you could speak to that. These IDPs that are scattered, and you put that in your testimony so that people who are already poor are taking on more, you know, desperately poor people and traumatized people at great sacrifice. So if you could speak so that, I would appreciate that.

And my second question would be on the budget. Is the budget sufficient? Are we providing enough? Do you feel that there are unmet needs that you would be doing if you had the money? Today, Ann Hollingsworth from Refugees International, will speak about her personal observations to the Sudanese refugee population in Chad. As she points out, in her view, it is an underreported story, and she goes to great lengths to talk about the cuts that WFP has made in early 2014, of a dramatic 50 percent cut, up to 60 percent in some areas, in food rations for Sudanese refugees in Chad.

She does point out later on about the self-reliance approach, which I think is a very innovative and good idea, provided there is an infrastructure that can accommodate that, and that is part of what her concern is, that there is not that infrastructure to accommodate a self-provided approach. If you could speak to that as well.

And then apparently we are not going to have votes until 4:30. So we are not as rushed as we thought we would be.

One of the areas that I think is absolutely transformational, I know you believe it as well, because USAID is totally committed to it, and that is the first 1,000 days of life from conception to the second birthday, and the scaling up programs that are going on. In Nigeria I have met and been to places, camps and to healthcare facilities, where stunting, and you know it, is a huge problem. And if the child and the mother get, as you know, sufficient supplementation, good nutritious foods, stunting almost goes away. Not in all cases. The child's immune system is bolstered big time, and I don't know if you know this, but I actually authored three laws on autism, including the Combating Autism Act, and most recently, the Autism CARES Act.

And three studies show that if a woman has folic acid in the first month of the pregnancy, after that it has an almost negligible impact, but the first month it brings down the risk factor of autism by 40 percent, which is absolutely transformational. As we know, WHO attests to, we are talking about tens of millions of kids, children, throughout Africa who are autistic and on the spectrum, and a very simple innovative inclusion. And I know Uganda and others have already supplemented, or put into their flour and other things, the right amount of folic acid.

So my question is about that first 1,000 days of life. In 2010, I met with seven first ladies of Africa at the U.N., and they gave powerful presentations, but they don't always have the where-withal to make sure that that unborn child and that mother, right until the second birthday, get the help they need. And then the next 25,000 to 30,000 days of that life will be exponentially improved, immune system strengthened, ability to resist malaria and its consequences. So I am wondering in the refugee population, the IDP population, what are we doing to scale up that first 1,000 days of life initiative?

Mr. STAAL. Thank you, Chairman Smith, for those questions. Critical questions, and, in fact, on your first question, working with faith-based organizations, just this morning I was actually on the panel over at the Religion and Sustainable Development, focusing on humanitarian assistance, meeting with a number of faith-based organizations.

That is an increasingly important part of the work there. Unfortunately, some of the conflicts in Africa are sectarian conflicts, and so the role of faith-based organizations has unique challenges, but unique strengths, and their strengths are that they have networks, they have credibility in the local community, they have systems to get out the word through their churches, mosques, and so on, and actually we have been—I don't say that maybe ''surprise'' is not the word, but happy to see that they are actually able to work together in many cases. You know, the case of Central African Republic where the Muslim imam, Catholic bishop and a Protestant leader have been working very closely together. In fact, the Islamic relief organization has their offices in the Catholic Relief Services (CRS) building. They provided offices for them. So you are seeing that. And increasingly, we are trying to work through those organizations. South Sudan is another major example of that where we have really reached out.

Now, they may also be involved in the conflict. So there are concerns of partiality. There are concerns sometimes that they are too closely linked with Western organizations. You know, it is good that Catholics have reached back through CRS, for instance, but on the other hand, sometimes local organizations say you are too closely linked. So that is something that they have to overcome and that we work with them on, and important to build that local capacity. But definitely, that is a major focus for what we are doing. I have met with the religious leaders in northern Nigeria from both sides as well, and they can play a crucial role there.

On your question about the budget, we have a robust budget thanks to Congress. We are the largest humanitarian assistance providers throughout Africa and the world. The needs are huge, as you and others have said and so we are increasingly looking, first of all, to make sure that every dollar is well spent, and then, are there ways that we can tweak our programs to make sure they are even more effective and more efficient?

Some of the food aid efficiencies that we have been able to do by some local purchase or vouchers have actually been able to reach 600,000 more people with the same amount of money over the last year because of that.

In the camps, Dadaab and Kakuma in Kenya, through working with UNHCR, they now do fingerprinting of all the refugees. That has reduced the number of beneficiaries by 20 percent, because there were a lot of people that shouldn't be getting the assistance or were double-counting and so on, and that is saving $1.5 million a month right there.

So, we are able to stretch those dollars. And then at the same time, we are working very closely with other donors to make sure they are upping their stuff, and with what you might call nontraditional donors.

I made a trip to Chad a few months ago with the Saudis, the Kuwaitis, the Emiratis and the Qataris to try to increase their support, not only in the Middle East, but also in Africa. So we are making some progress, but it is a huge demand, and I think we also need to go to more creative methods. Such as how do we get the private sector to be more involved? In the Central African Republic, we have a peace partnership bringing in the private sector, but I think it is not just about corporate social responsibility. We need to find ways to make it attractive for investment in those communities, and I think that is something that is a challenge for us and the international community to work on.

Mr. SMITH. On that first 1,000 days, is that——

Mr. STAAL. On the first 1,000 days—yes. Thank you. That is so critical.

That is part of the reason that we have recently, over the last couple of years, put a lot of thinking and research to develop improved products, especially for those young children in the first month and in the first year. With these ready-to-use supplemental foods and ready-to-use therapeutic foods, we have redone our famous CSB, the corn/soy blend, so that it is now more fortified with the right kind of vitamins and minerals, especially addressing the kids at that age, and working, not only through our humanitarian programs, but through Feed the Future and some of our agriculture programs, to make sure that countries are properly fortifying the flour that goes through their normal commercial sectors. There is iron fortification and other types of things to address some of those very issues. Critical. Thank you.

Ms. WIESNER. I think my colleague Tom has said most of it, but just to add on the question of working with religious communities, when I was in South Sudan at the IDP site inside the UNMISS peacekeeping base in Bor, I met with a pastor who was still in touch with his colleagues of other ethnicities who were living outside of that base, and the level of violence between communities in South Sudan has been so shocking, but it is heartening when you find people like that who are determined to overcome that violence. And a number of the religious leaders who actually have resided inside these camps have been helpful in mitigating some of the intercommunal tension. So, part of the increasing focus on recognizing the role of frontline humanitarian responders has been that the first people usually to provide aid are from within local communities they are from the country themselves.

Even the national staff of some of the international organizations that we fund are, in fact, from those communities. And so I think making sure that we understand the important role they play and invest in that is quite important.

On the budget, Tom has also said it, but there is no question that this is an extraordinary period of humanitarian need, and that the resources are not keeping pace, but I think the bottom line is that the U.S. Congress has been generous and that the U.S. is generally paying its fair share. So I think the partnership that we could form would be to do some of this outreach that Tom has talked about to other states, to the private sector, even for private giving. A lot of the money that is raised from private individual donors generally goes toward natural disasters, which is really important and wonderful, but we would like to see if we can increase that type of interest in some of these conflict-related situations and bring more donors into the field.

Mr. SMITH. Thank you.

Ranking Member Bass.

Ms. BASS. Thank you very much, Mr. Chair. A few questions I wanted to ask you, I was thinking about what you were saying in terms of the first 1,000 days, and it made me think of how difficult it is, frankly, to be pregnant here in Washington, DC, if you are poor, let alone in an IDP camp. So I wanted to know what we were doing in terms of family planning for those women who do not want to be pregnant because they are in a refugee camp, and, you know, whether it is direct U.S. dollars or U.S. collaborating with NGOs. What are we doing to provide family planning services in IDP camps?

Mr. STAAL. It is so critical to provide all the options for the local women in terms of family planning for those who want it. When I was working in Ethiopia, I visited not only local communities, but the IDP camps. Often they are living in the local community, to improve the skills, if you will, of the local health providers so that they can counsel young women on what their options are, and then provide those services at the community level. It used to be you had to go all the way to a hospital. Now, in many of these coun-

24

tries, through our interventions, they are able to provide that at the local community level.

Ms. BASS. But what about in the IDP camp? Are you referring to IDP—when you say ''community,'' you are referring to the camp itself? So while we provide the food assistance and all, I am just wondering, in the camp?

Mr. STAAL. Yes. Through our food assistance and through our healthcare assistance, we then also provide various family planning methods to the women. First the counseling on what their options are, and then the actual——

Ms. BASS. Birth control?

Mr. STAAL. Birth control, condoms, things like that.

Ms. BASS. Okay. Thank you.

Ms. WIESNER. And we also support UNFPA which provides reproductive health services to displaced people, and they have been working on improving their emergency services to make those available sooner in an emergency including for adolescents.

Ms. BASS. So I was thinking about, you know, every few days on the news, we see the folks who are dying at sea leaving Libya and going to Europe, and I was wondering what kind of collaboration are we doing?

Ms. WIESNER. Well, first of all, two of our key partners, the U.N. Refugee Agency and the International Organization for Migration, are highly engaged in this challenge. And so we do support both of those organizations to work with countries of origin, with countries of first asylum, with countries of transit, and as well as the work they do in Europe where people arrive. So, one of our priorities is to promote the role that they play because they operate based on a set of very important humanitarian principles.

But it is a very complex challenge. Migration is not something that can be stopped. It is not something that necessarily should be stopped. People who are fleeing violence and persecution need to have the opportunity to seek protection. Even people who are just seeking better economic opportunity for their families will always continue to do so, and, in fact, can be a benefit to the societies that they travel to.

The challenge is in making that migration safe and orderly, and so, I think that is what Europe is grappling with right now is how to create more legal avenues for migration, how to crack down on unscrupulous smugglers who take advantage of people, and also, to address the root causes that are causing people who would not otherwise choose to move from doing so. And that is a responsibility, I think, of the global community because of the humanitarian dimensions of this crisis. But it also is a very specific responsibility of states, because ultimately, immigration laws and policy are the responsibilities of states. What we always advocate at PRM, from a humanitarian perspective, is that human rights must be respected, even as countries seek to implement laws and secure their borders.

Ms. BASS. You know, you mentioned 19,000 African refugees in the United States. Where are they?

Ms. WIESNER. Where are they coming from or where are they going to?

Ms. BASS. Both, actually.

Ms. WIESNER. So 29 different nationalities benefit from that program, which means they are coming from all over the continent.

Ms. BASS. So are they connecting—when they come to the United States, are they connecting with family? We have had the situations in the past whether they were refugees from Somalia or other countries or the Sudan, so is it that type of situation where they are not connected to family here or they are?

Ms. WIESNER. It is both. And Somalia is one of the largest populations that we do resettle, and some of them are coming to join family who have come previously; others are coming purely based on their own claims to asylum.

Ms. BASS. Could you list a few other countries? Like the top five, maybe, would be helpful.

Ms. WIESNER. We will get back to you with the precise figures on the top five.

[The information referred to follows:]

WRITTEN RESPONSE RECEIVED FROM MS. CATHERINE WIESNER TO QUESTION ASKED DURING THE HEARING BY THE HONORABLE KAREN BASS

In FY 2014, the top five African nationalities admitted to the United States through the Refugee Admissions Program for resettlement and the number of refugees for those nationalities were:
1. Somali—9,000
2. DR Congolese—4,540
3. Eritrea—1,488
4. Sudanese—1,315
5. Ethiopia—728

Ms. BASS. And then I can't remember which one of you mentioned providing psychosocial—I think it was you, Mr. Staal—mentioned providing psychosocial services. And were you referring to Nigeria?

Mr. STAAL. Yes.

Ms. BASS. So who are the providers and how is that done?

Mr. STAAL. It is a combination of organizations—some of them are U.N., like UNICEF, especially for children who are affected, either directly through the release from captivity, or just from the displacement, and then some of our NGOs as well. In fact, we make sure that every grant that we provide through our OFDA programs includes the protection aspect as a component.

Ms. BASS. And are they social workers? Do you know what kind of providers they are?

Mr. STAAL. It is a combination of things. Most of them are probably not trained social workers. Some of them are, but there is a lot of other things too. Even things like we provide what we call safe spaces for the children in the IDP or refugee camps, so that there is a tent that is just for children to go and play, and maybe have some kindergarten——

Ms. BASS. I am just curious as to how they deal with all the different cultures that they encounter, you know. What kind of backgrounds and training that they——

Mr. STAAL. It is critical to involve the local community themselves, and find people in the community that you can provide some training, maybe they already have some, and work with them to help to bridge that gap. Yes, so critical.

26

Ms. BASS. And then, finally, you were talking about our involvement in CAR, and you were talking about the conflict, the Muslim/Christian conflict, and are we involved in any conflict resolution? And we are able to fund faith-based organizations directly. Correct?

Mr. STAAL. Yes.

Ms. BASS. We fund both Christian and Muslim?

Mr. STAAL. Yes. Thank you very much. In CAR, we have several programs that are definitely focused on conflict prevention, youth engagement, and directly involving faith-based organizations, both Christian and Muslim, primarily through international organizations that have international faith-based or Western or Muslim groups who then have local groups that they work through there.

Ms. BASS. Thank you.

Mr. STAAL. And we are seeing some real positive movement there. Thanks.

Ms. BASS. Excellent.

Mr. SMITH. Thank you.

Mr. Cicilline.

Mr. CICILLINE. Thank you. Thank you, Mr. Chairman. Thank you to our witnesses. I think as was mentioned, we are living at a time of really unprecedented refugee and displaced persons. I think the number is close to 60 million, according to the United Nations. And you spoke a little bit about what we are doing, both what the U.S. is doing and what we are encouraging others to do, and in light of the magnitude of the challenge, is the United States doing enough? Should we be doing more? Are there additional things we could be doing to support the refugees and internally displaced persons? And at the same time, what success are you having? You said you have been in conversations with some potentially new donors. I think the last report by the U.N. was that if you look at the humanitarian crisis in Syria, Iraq, South Sudan, Yemen, Somalia, and a few others places, that international donors so far are only providing about 26 percent of the need, which means obviously three-quarters of the need is not being met. Would you talk a little more about the conversations that are being had with other countries and the likelihood that they will do their part in responding to this crisis in different places around the world?

Mr. STAAL. Thank you, Mr. Cicilline. An important question. As I said, the need is so huge, and there is a combination of things, and we have seen some positive movement from, especially the Middle Eastern countries. As I mentioned, I was in Chad, and as a follow-up to that, I know that several of them have now put some money into supporting some efforts in Chad. In Somalia, actually, they are doing quite a bit of work with local organizations. Part of the issue is we don't always know what they are doing, and a big issue is trying to sort of help them to understand the need to co-operate, with the coordination systems that other international donors work with in.

So we have a cooperation now with the Organization of Islamic Cooperation to build their networks. They have asked for training. They want to understand the system better and work with us more closely. So that is a critical aspect.

And on the first part of your question, trying to address those psychosocial needs are so important. Actually, there is an interagency group called the Atrocity Prevention Board. Maybe you have heard of it, chaired by the NSC and involving a number of U.S. agencies in helping us to make sure that that is an important aspect in all these situations, looking at our U.S. Government efforts and making sure that we are doing that. This has helped us to get support for those kind of efforts in CAR and in other countries, and to marshal our resources and efforts in a coordinated fashion across the interagency.

Mr. CICILLINE. So if I could just follow up on Ms. Bass' question with respect to the psychosocial services. I mean, we have spent a lot of time focused on the necessities of food and water and shelter, but would you speak a little bit about the unmet need as it relates to more of the kind of counseling and mental health interventions and psychosocial services because—particularly children are coming from horrific unspeakable experiences of violence, and feeding them and being sure they are housed and have clothing is a base, but there are obviously huge needs. Would you speak a little bit about what the level of unmet need is in that area and what we could be doing better?

Mr. STAAL. That is such a critical question. In any disaster situation, people become more vulnerable to all kinds of predators, to— vulnerable to a number of protection issues, especially women and children. But, unfortunately, one of the phenomenon of the recent events in Africa, as I mentioned, is more related to sectarian and ethic violence and terrorist violence rather than just natural disasters. And we are finding that those issues of atrocities, especially against women and children, are worse than ever, and so we are having to increase our efforts. That is why, as I mentioned, all of our OFDA grants include protection as a feature of what we are trying to do, especially counseling for children who have been affected.

UNICEF is the main provider there, but Save the Children, obviously, and other organizations that we work with. Gender-based violence is such a huge problem. We are seeing in South Sudan, you have probably seen some of the U.N. reports and so on that it seems to be done not just drunken soldiers, but really a systematic process of atrocities. I think we saw that years ago in the Balkans as well. And when you have these kind of sectarian or ethnic issues, it becomes even worse.

Ms. WIESNER. I would add in terms of the question of unmet needs, that I think one of the areas where we have really seen some ground lost is in the inclusion of education services for all ages of children, preschool, primary, and secondary education, when they are in situations of displacement, when budgets are stretched, and as you said, the focus tends to then go toward very, very basic lifesaving activities, education doesn't always make the cut. And that is really something that I think is disheartening to the humanitarian organizations themselves. They want to be able to provide those services. They know the importance of it for everything from psychosocial support to the future for these populations for the countries that they come from, education is critical, and I would certainly put that in the category of one of the often unmet needs.

28

Mr. CICILLINE. Thank you very much. I yield back, Mr. Chairman.

Mr. SMITH. Just a couple of follow-up questions. On the question that I posed earlier about Chad, again, Ann Hollingsworth makes an impassioned plea, including in her recommendations that donors and WFP must immediately increase food rations to 2,100 kilocalories per day for vulnerable Sudanese refugees, until such time as assistance can be adjusted in line with region-wide households, economic assessments. And, again, she talks about having just been there along with Michael Boyce, her colleague, and I am wondering what we are doing vis-à-vis that situation, if you could be specific?

Secondly, you mentioned, Mr. Staal, about the Atrocities Prevention Board, and, of course, the international community, including and especially the United States and the U.N. missed it with Rwanda when the genocide could have been mitigated, maybe even stopped, years ago. Infamously missed it. The famous facts. I held hearings on it at the time, and soon thereafter.

Yesterday I had a bill on the floor on Srebrenica, and I actually had the translator at one of my hearings in the 1990s who was there when the Dutch peacekeepers gave over to Mladić the okay to take out some 6,000 Muslim men, and 8,000, of course, were slaughtered within a 4-day time period, and the 20th anniversary for that, as we all know, is on July 11, and I have been to re-interment ceremonies at Srebrenica, moved to tears by the families who lost loved ones, who were butchered and killed simply because they were Muslims. It was genocide. And that is what our resolution reiterated again yesterday.

But it brings me to your point, Mr. Staal, about the Atrocities Prevention Board, which sounds good and may be doing a wonderful job, but as we all know, according to UNHCR, in the 2014 Global Trends report in the past 5 years, at least 15 significant conflicts have started, or re-ignited worldwide. And eight of those have been in Africa, as you know, and both of you know so well. And I am wondering, you know, what role the Atrocities Prevention Board is playing. We are planning a hearing to hear about that sometime in the latter part of September. We will ask them to give us a sense of what kind of day-to-day work they do. But maybe you could shed some light on that.

And finally, the TIP Report. As you may know, I am of the author of the Trafficking Victims Protection Act of 2000 which created our strategy, our landmark effort to prevent, prosecute, and protect, protect the victims, of course. The TIP Report is a month late, and I am always worried when it is late, because it may be because Secretary Kerry broke his leg and wants to personally unveil it. And he is a little busy in Iran.

But, again, there are multi-taskers and there are people who could take—I am always worried, especially with regards to this hearing, every refugee camp, IDP camp I ever go to, I ask questions about trafficking and what is in place to ensure that no young girls or boys, or women, even, in their 20s or 30s are trafficked into a horrible outcome. And I am wondering if you could speak to that effort, because I know you are doing much on it. You always do.

But just if you could elaborate and provide some insights to the subcommittee, particularly with all these new IDPs and refugees.

And before that, I do want to note that Albert Puela is with us today. He is Member of Parliament from the DR Congo. I met Albert on our way to Goma several years ago looking into, you know, the peacekeeping effort there. But Albert is a Member and he won reelection, and Albert, thank you for joining us.

Please, if you could answer the——

Ms. WIESNER. Yeah. I will say a few words about Chad and then turn it over to Tom who has been there. It is an excellent report from Refugees International, I think, because it lays out the challenges. Chad is a somewhat unique situation. Sometimes it is politically sensitive to promote self-reliance of refugees, because it raises questions about land access, the right to work, vis-à-vis local populations, and a host of other issues. In Chad, the government is actually quite keen for refugees to become self-reliant, and it is more a challenge of the environment, the development funding, the development actors. So it is important also to recognize that some of these protracted issues are very context-specific in terms of what the solutions are.

On trafficking, thank you for asking those questions, every time you go to camps because we ask the same ones. And it is certainly part of the protection role of UNHCR and other actors who work there to ensure that children and vulnerable populations are not trafficked out of camps, are not recruited into armed groups, and any number of other threats that could face them. So thank you for raising those questions when you do travel.

Mr. STAAL. Thank you very much. As I mentioned, I was in Chad a few months ago and visited a couple of places around the country, including the southern area where the refugees were coming across from the Central African Republic. Chad remains, actually, a pretty large beneficiary of our Food for Peace Program. We have been putting normally over $50 million a year worth of food aid there and some other humanitarian assistance. And we continue to stay committed to that. So that is going to be important. But as you say, at some point, the refugees need to find a way to either go back home, but if that is not possible, to find a way to become part of the local economy.

The Atrocities Prevention Board, what we have been able to do is then bring all the U.S. agencies together to focus on an issue. So, for instance, in the CAR, where we don't have a USAID mission, we were able to get support for some of our conflict prevention and youth engagement programs working with faith-based organizations. We got support for that across the interagency, and then were able to use some of the funds that were generously provided by Congress for a country where we don't normally have an aid program.

In Burundi in 2013, we saw that this was going to be a difficult place and that things were not going in the right way. So, again, we were able to put in additional resources there toward things like youth engagement especially, some civil society support, and help with developing their election system. Now, that doesn't mean you won't have a guy who is going to try to run for president even though—the term limit issue. But the technically the election system is working much better.

So those kinds of things with the Atrocity Prevention Board, we are able to get support to do some of those kind of things that we think are critical.

Mr. SMITH. Thank you.

Mr. Clawson.

Mr. CLAWSON. Sorry I was late. We get to be double-booked here, so sometimes it is hard to get everywhere at once. So I am sorry I missed your opening. Certainly no disrespect in any way.

I want to ask a general question, and then I will let you all continue with the train of thought that you have had here. When I think about Africa, all the displaced because of these wars, because of dictators, layered in with all the disease and other things that we have to fight with, and then masses of people heading north, and we see them, you know, you go to northern Spain, you see them in the plaza. I mean, you see them everywhere. Right? Because folks are trying to get where they are safe and can eat. We all understand that.

And, but we are Americans. We are way over here. USAID, you know, is on site. State Departmentis working. Do we have influence to change the course here? I mean, on a general level? Are we secondary to Europe here, or can we really play the lead and can we get the herd moving in a different direction, or are we just fighting to tread water? Does my question make sense to you all? Is this winnable, or do—or is this winnable only by the Europeans, I guess?

Ms. WIESNER. So we did address this a bit, and I think the first——

Mr. CLAWSON. And I apologize for the repetition.

Ms. WIESNER. That is okay. No, the first thing to say is that migration has existed forever, and will continue to do so. I think what is so concerning today is the scale, the nature of that migration, the number of deaths that we are seeing. We learn about the deaths when we know about boats drowning in the Mediterranean. There are also people dying in the desert before they ever get to the shores of Libya, and we don't see a lot of that.

I was in Niger recently, and there is a town in the north of Niger called Agadez, where the International Organization for Migration predicts 100,000 people will move through that town this year on their way to Libya. And this is an impoverished country that is already hosting refugees from Nigeria and Mali, and is now sort of the target of attention from Europe and elsewhere as a very important transit point. It has, again, historically, throughout the years, been an important crossroads for trade and migration. And, in fact, west Africa has freedom of movement. So it is not illegal to travel to Niger. What is illegal is to be smuggled into Algeria or Libya and then across the Mediterranean. So all this to say it is a very complicated challenge, and certainly those whose are fleeing from war and persecution need to be able to do so and need to be able to find protection.

I think what some of our investments do, and can do, and do do, is improve the situation for people in their home countries and in their countries of first asylum. When people leave Eritrea for Ethiopia, they should have some opportunity to make a life for themselves and we have worked very hard on improving the conditions of camps there. The option to travel across the sea should not be the only one that they see for themselves.

But you also, when you interview those migrants, find that some of them are paying huge amounts of money, actually, to take those journeys. They are saving up thousands and thousands of dollars to be able to take that risk on behalf of their families.

Mr. CLAWSON. Can I jump in just for a second. Do the Spaniards, French, and Italians, among others, see it the same way as what you just explained?

Ms. WIESNER. Well, the European Union is a collection of member states, and we—so I think you have, you know, a very wide range of views within the European Union. There are certain states that are quite generous in accepting refugees for resettlement that provide great benefits to those who arrive in their countries, and others who have different policies. We do have a policy dialogue with the European Union. We call it the Platform on Refugees, Asylum, and Migration, where we get together regularly to discuss at the diplomatic and the policy level, and compare notes.

We are also a destination country for migration here in the United States, and it is a different set of conditions and a different, you know, group of people that are seeking to reach the United States. But there are some similarities in figuring out how you can appropriately secure your borders, but also allow those who are seeking protection to have the opportunity to do so.

So we are engaged in dialogue with the European Union, but we also see that there is a certain prerogative that they have to address this situation. We do urge always that they work with the U.N. Refugee Agency, with the International Organization for Migration, and other groups that can assist them with best practices in handling migration challenges.

Mr. STAAL. Thank you, Mr. Clawson. Part of the issue that we are trying to address from the USAID side is the root causes of the migration. You are not going to stop everybody. As Catherine was saying, migration and refugees have gone on forever. But a lot of those drivers of the displacement are rooted in the local community. Sometimes it is economic. It is political. It is violence. It is a number of other things. So a lot of our programs are trying to help with conflict mitigation, and again with youth engagement. A lot of it involves young people who are not finding jobs. So partly, it is to give them a sense of hope that there is something going on.

And, you know, that is economic issues and so on. It is also good governance. What we are finding is most of this displacement happens from fragile states. And the way we define fragility is, number one, the ability of the government to provide services, whatever it is supposed to provide, everything from electricity and water and schools and security. But it is also the legitimacy and the credibility of the government. It is those two factors.

So a huge part of our program is to try to address those drivers of fragility that will then hopefully reduce the lure of extremism and the desire for people to leave and find something else.

Mr. CLAWSON. So if leadership is not trustworthy and equitable, which means opportunity for everyone, then we are really fighting an uphill battle here, and when the rich get everything and everybody else gets nothing, then why stay? But what I hear you saying is, you know, we are working at humanitarian level and a governance level, and what I am saying is if the Europeans don't get in the game on that, then it just feels like a long putt for Americans to solve problems, and I am, on how you all describe the issues, having been to a lot of these countries, I think I agree, and certainly admire what you all do, and the kinds of sacrifices your folks make for this region.

Mr. STAAL. Thank you very much. It continues to be an issue, but the Europeans are involved. Right after this hearing I am heading up to New York to meet with the Brits and the EU and several of the other Europeans, in this case specifically about Yemen, but a similar issue, and we meet regularly about issues in Africa as well. So they are involved.

Mr. CLAWSON. Are they doing their fair share?

Ms. WIESNER. What I was going to add, we are certainly the lead humanitarian donor in the world. I oversee our international migration policy office at PRM, and in these dialogues that we have had over the last few years with the European Union, I think what we have seen is that other parts of the Commission that have responsibility for home affairs, for immigration policy, have started to realize that their investments in Africa and other sources of migration need to go beyond just law enforcement, and address some of the same root causes that Tom was talking about.

And that is what has been really interesting, and, you know, there was a $1 billion trust fund recently established by the European Union, and when I talked to the head of their mission in Niger and said: Is this going to go beyond just counter-smuggling and trafficking, which is important, to address some of the root causes and create opportunities for people in their home countries, they said that is certainly the intent.

So I think you are seeing an evolution in the thinking, too, as the problem has gotten so much larger and more visible to really try to understand the complexity of it and realize that it requires more investment on various fronts.

Mr. CLAWSON. Thank you for letting me have so much time. I yield back.

Mr. SMITH. Thank you, Mr. Clawson.

Ms. Bass.

Ms. BASS. Thank you.

You know, sometimes I don't feel like we put enough pressure on the EU. Because if you are going to talk about root causes, I mean, you are talking about their former colonies. And they have a level of responsibility to this, and they don't step up enough. And it seems like, to me, we need to put a little extra pressure.

Anyway, I neglected to ask about African refugees who have been going into Israel. And I wanted to know, one, if you could speak to that and to what extent we are working with the Israeli Government.

I was recently in Israel in May, and, at that point, when I was there, it was an issue. And I am not referring to Ethiopians. I am referring to other African countries where there is a growing ref-

ugee problem in Israel and how we might be working with the
Israeli Government around that.

Ms. WIESNER. Sure. Yes. So, previously, we had been quite focused on the situation of sub-Saharan Africans moving through the
Sinai to Israel and how they were both treated in the Sinai and
received in Israel. When a wall was built on that border, that particular phenomenon has subsided somewhat.

But we have continued to receive reports and express our concern to the Government of Israel about the treatment of sub-Saharan Africa asylum seekers in Israel. Both the detention practices
as well as the accessibility of the asylum system are two things
that have been part of an ongoing dialogue with that government.

Ms. BASS. What countries are they coming from, and how are
they held? I mean, I have seen a couple of photographs, but I don't
know much about it. It is not talked about very much. There is not
a lot of news coverage about this.

Ms. WIESNER. My understanding is that it is a lot from the Horn
of Africa—Somalis, Ethiopians, and Eritreans, among others.

Ms. BASS. And do you know in what kind of situations they are
in? Do you know what I mean? Is it a camp? Is it like an IDP
camp? Or what is the physical setting? And do you have any idea
on the numbers?

Ms. WIESNER. We will definitely get back to you with the numbers.

[The information referred to follows:]

WRITTEN RESPONSE RECEIVED FROM MS. CATHERINE WIESNER TO QUESTION ASKED
DURING THE HEARING BY THE HONORABLE KAREN BASS

According to the Population and Immigration Authority (PIBA) of Israel's Ministry of Interior, as of April 1, 2015, Eritrean and Sudanese nationals constituted
92 percent of the 45,711 individuals seeking asylum and refugee status in Israel.
These individuals have been classified in official Israeli government documents as
''infiltrators''. Of these, 33,506 (73 percent) are from Eritrea, while 8,637 are from
Sudan (19 percent). In addition, there are 2,984 individuals from the rest of Africa;
their countries of origin are not delineated by PIBA, but past groups seeking protection in Israel have includes those from the Cote d'Ivoire and the Democratic Republic of Congo.

Ms. WIESNER. Most migrants and asylum seekers live in cities.
There aren't really camps. But there has been a problem of detention of——

Ms. BASS. So maybe that is what I am referring to, because what
I saw was not a city.

Ms. WIESNER. It was probably one of the detention facilities.

Ms. BASS. Okay.

Thank you.

Mr. SMITH. I do have one final question. When it comes to U.N.
humanitarian appeals, UNHCR appeals and the like, have you de-
tected any diversion of prioritization for African crises, especially
with Syria, Iraq, ISIS, Yemen? And you will be talking about
Yemen at the U.N. very shortly. Is that diverting money and
prioritization away from these other crises? Is there a relative loss
of capacity because of that?

Mr. STAAL. That is a difficult question. I don't know that I have
seen diversion, but, certainly, the multiplicity and the demands
across the world are having an impact everywhere. But I haven't

34

seen that they are getting a higher percentage of their appeals than other countries. But it is a huge demand across the world.

Mr. SMITH. But even as those appeals are formulated—and I have had conversations with UNHCR for 30 years on this, over 30 years—they have a need, but they also do an expectation about what they think they might be able to get, rather than just going with the need, and then if they fall short, at least they tried for what they truly needed.

So I do worry that we never know what the real calculation would have been had it been all needs-based, I would just say.

Mr. STAAL. I know that is an important factor that we have to look at.

Ms. WIESNER. Yeah, we have also had this dialogue on going with UNHCR, and they do now do needs-based budgeting, so there is a sense of, you know, what the full scope of the needs are against what they are receiving.

But you are right; because they don't ever receive the full amount that they feel they need, they have to make decisions about what to allocate to different country operations, and that can be hard. It is why they appeal for as much flexible funding as possible, to be able to balance out between different areas.

Mr. SMITH. Thank you.

Anything else you want to add?

If our subcommittee could be of any help, please let us know, and we will do our level-best.

Mr. STAAL. Thank you very much.

Ms. WIESNER. Thank you very much for this hearing. Thank you.

Mr. SMITH. Thank you.

I would like to now welcome our second panel to the witness table, beginning with, first, Mr. John Stauffer, who served with the Peace Corps in Eritrea from 1966 to 1968, teaching English and science to rural middle school students there. In 2003, after the worst of the repression within Eritrea, he joined with one of his star Peace Corps students, who was an asylee, and founded a group called The America Team for Displaced Eritreans, which was established in 2010. He now assists Eritrean refugees and asylum seekers in the U.S. and around the world through resettlement services, policy advocacy, and lifesaving interventions.

We will then hear from Ms. Ann Hollingsworth, who joined Refugees International in January 2014. In her role as senior advocate for government relations, she leads Refugees International's advocacy efforts within the U.S. foreign policy community. Previously, she represented the International Crisis Group at Washington policy audiences. She provided political and strategic analysis and covered all crisis group areas of reporting, with primary responsibility for advocacy and research for the Africa portfolio. She has been a panelist at a variety of foreign policy events, including with the State Department, Brookings Institution, and the Tom Lantos Human Rights Commission. She also served in the office of U.S. Senator Ernest Hollings.

We will then hear from Ms. Natalie Eisenbarth of the International Rescue Committee, who is a policy and advocacy officer at the IRC, based right here in Washington. In this capacity, she leads IRC's policy and advocacy toward the U.S. Government on issues related to the organization's work in sub-Saharan Africa. Ms. Eisenbarth focuses specifically on humanitarian responses in South Sudan, Central African Republic, Somalia, and Kenya. She has completed research and factfinding missions in South Sudan, CAR, DR Congo, Kenya, Liberia, Sierra Leone, and Mali. Prior to joining the IRC, she worked at InterAction, facilitating its policy advocacy on international humanitarian missions.

Ms. BASS. May I say a word?

Mr. SMITH. Sure. I yield to Ms. Bass.

Ms. BASS. Thank you.

I just wanted to acknowledge that we have been joined by Nokuthula Sithole. She is Miss South Africa USA, and she is running for Miss Africa USA. I just wanted to acknowledge her being here.

Thank you.

Mr. SMITH. And we are joined by Congressman Mark Meadows of the subcommittee.

Mr. Meadows?

Mr. MEADOWS. Mr. Chairman, thank you for your leadership on this effort and continuing to highlight what for many of us is just an unbelievable travesty and difficult thing to swallow. I mean, I know for me and my family this particular issue has been something that dates back some 25 years. And so I just fully support you, not only in this effort, but thank each of the witnesses for being here.

Certainly, your testimony goes a long ways to touching even children. Both my son and my daughter getting involved really came from hearing compelling testimony that happened right here on Capitol Hill many years ago. And so, hopefully, young people will get engaged and continue to fight for those that, many times, they can't fight for themselves.

So thank you. Thank you, Mr. Chairman. And look forward to your testimony.

Mr. SMITH. Mr. Stauffer?

STATEMENT OF MR. JOHN STAUFFER, PRESIDENT, THE AMERICA TEAM FOR DISPLACED ERITREANS

Mr. STAUFFER. Thank you, Mr. Chairman and subcommittee members and staff, for conducting this important hearing, and I am honored to participate today.

Again, I am John Stauffer. I am president of The America Team for Displaced Eritreans, which is a small, U.S.-based nonprofit that assists refugees and asylum seekers from Eritrea, located in northeast Africa. We maintain a Web site at EritreanRefugees.org.

Many years ago, I was a teacher in Eritrea with the U.S. Peace Corps. And now, for the past 11 years, I have, along with other team members, assisted Eritrean refugees fleeing acute oppression and abuse in their country. I can also speak toward the situation as it stands in Israel.

As part of our work, we seek assistance and protection for individuals or groups of refugees in dangerous situations when we are contacted by victims or their relatives. We have helped refugees in at least 15 different countries in Africa and elsewhere. We operate by alerting and then working closely with UNHCR, pertinent local

NGOs, local government officials, or other Eritreans, any of whom may be able to help the refugees on an urgent basis. We also assist Eritrean refugees who are here in the United States.

Eritrea is a police state, often referred to as the North Korea of Africa. On June 8 of this year, the U.N. Human Rights Council released a 480-plus-page report on human rights offenses conducted in the country since independence in 1993.

In Eritrea, there is extensive, abusive, essentially unpaid, endless military conscription, often characterized by survivors as slave labor. Soldiers accused of any infraction or dissatisfaction are often tortured. There is total lack of basic human rights, almost no freedom to worship or to congregate, no free speech, and no public media. There is ongoing surveillance, threats, and intimidation and abuse of the families of those who flee the country. And there is acute and extensive torture of those who are imprisoned.

So it is no wonder that, as a consequence of those conditions, thousands of citizens, mostly young people and often unaccompanied children, flee the country every month. Initial destinations of flight from Eritrea include Ethiopia to the south, where about 100,000 Eritrean refugees now reside, primarily in refugee camps, most surviving with little to do and no hope for the future, and Sudan to the west, where there are also refugee camps, plus many urban refugees. Here, life is equally hopeless, and kidnappers and human traffickers lie in wait.

Sudan, in particular, is often the starting point for new and horrific ordeals. Eritrean security police operate freely in eastern Sudan and in Khartoum and seek out and haul back to Eritrea high-value targets such as government officials and military offi- cers who have sought refuge. The refugees may be kidnapped and extorted locally for a few thousand dollars or taken off to Egypt or Libya, where they are abused.

In 2007, Eritreans were paying smugglers to move them across Egypt to the Israel border, where thousands entered with the hope for asylum. But, by 2009, a system of human trafficking developed, not for servitude, but for the purpose of torture, for extortion of huge amounts of money. Groups of refugees would be either double-crossed by their paid smugglers or be kidnapped in Sudan and then be trucked into Egypt and sold to rogue Egyptian Bedouins and end up in torture camps in northern Sinai.

The refugees would be tortured continuously and mercilessly to extract ransom from their impoverished families in Eritrea or in other countries. As torture, molten plastic from burning bottles and bags would be dripped onto bare skin, causing excruciating pain. Victims were tied and left on the ground under the blazing sun. They were burned with cigarettes and electroshock. Women were continually raped, often gang-raped, and men were raped as well. Victims were threatened with extraction of body parts.

The victims were forced to call relatives by cell phone, and then they were tortured while on the phone so their relatives could hear their screams. The torture business became more lucrative, and typical ransoms grew from a few thousand dollars to at least $30,000 per person. Relatives who managed to raise the funds became impoverished for life.

When the Morsi government in Egypt fell in 2013, the Egyptian Army restored its presence in northern Sinai, and the atrocities against the Eritrean refugees abated there.

We learned recently at a conference in Geneva with UNHCR that 7,000 Sinai torture survivors are presently in Israel. But kidnapping, extortion, and torture of Eritrean refugees continue to occur in Sudan, Libya, and possibly other parts of Sinai. Still, there seems to be little governmental effort in Sudan and Libya to stop it. To the contrary, corrupt security officials often know of the traffic and torture yet look the other way.

Finally, tragically, many Eritrean refugees are torture survivors, from their time in Eritrea or from the period of their flight or both.

Thank you, Mr. Chairman, again, for considering these observations.

[The prepared statement of Mr. Stauffer follows:]

TESTIMONY:

WITNESS: JOHN G. STAUFFER
PRESIDENT, THE AMERICA TEAM FOR DISPLACED ERITREANS (EIN 27-2142524)
BEFORE: THE HOUSE COMMITTEE ON FOREIGN AFFAIRS
JULY 9, 2015: *AFRICA'S DISPLACED PEOPLE*
HELD BY: THE HOUSE SUBCOMMITTEE ON AFRICA, GLOBAL HEALTH, GLOBAL
      HUMAN RIGHTS, AND INTERNATIONAL ORGANIZATIONS

Mr. Chairman, my oral testimony is essentially set forth as the first part of my written testimony.

Thank you, Mr. Chairman, and Subcommittee members and staff, for conducting this important hearing. I'm honored to participate today.

I am John Stauffer, president of The America Team for Displaced Eritreans, which is a small US-based nonprofit that assists refugees and asylum seekers from Eritrea, located in northeast Africa.

We maintain a web site at EritreanRefugees.org.

Many years ago I was a teacher in Eritrea with the U.S. Peace Corps. And now, for the past 11 years, I have, along with other Team members, assisted Eritrean refugees fleeing acute oppression and abuse in their country.

As part of our work, we seek assistance and protection for individuals or groups of refugees in dangerous situations, when we are contacted by victims or their relatives. We have helped refugees in at least 15 different countries in Africa, and elsewhere. We operate by alerting and then working closely with UNHCR, pertinent local NGOs, local government officials, or other Eritreans, any of whom may be able to help the refugees on an urgent basis.

We also assist Eritrean refugees who are in need in the United States.

Eritrea is a police state, often referred to as the "North Korea of Africa." On June 8th of this year, the UN Human Rights Council released a 480-page report on human rights offenses conducted in the country since independence in 1993.

In Eritrea, there is extensive, abusive, essentially unpaid endless military conscription – often characterized by survivors as slave labor. Soldiers accused of any infraction or dissatisfaction are often tortured. There is total lack of basic human rights: almost no freedom to worship or to congregate; no free speech, no public media. There is ongoing surveillance, threats and intimidation; and abuse of the families of those who flee the country. And there is acute and extensive torture of those who are imprisoned.

It is no wonder that, as a consequence of those conditions, thousands of citizens – mostly young people and often unaccompanied children – flee the country every month. Initial destinations of flight from Eritrea include:

- **Ethiopia**, to the south, where about 100,000 Eritrean refugees now reside, primarily in refugee camps, most surviving with little to do and no hope for the future.
- **Sudan**, to the west, where there are also refugee camps, plus many urban refugees – here, life is equally hopeless, and kidnappers and human traffickers lie in wait.

Sudan in particular is often the starting point for new and horrific ordeals:

- Eritrean security police operate freely in eastern Sudan and in Khartoum, and seek out and haul back to Eritrea, high value targets, such as government officials and military officers who have sought refuge.
- The refugees may be kidnapped and extorted locally for a few thousand dollars, or taken off to Egypt or Libya where they are abused.

In 2007, Eritreans were paying smugglers to move them across Egypt to the Israel border, where thousands entered with a hope for asylum. But by 2009, a system of human trafficking developed... not for servitude, but for the purpose of torture for extortion of huge amounts of money.

Groups of refugees would be either double-crossed by their paid smugglers, or be kidnapped in Sudan, and then be trucked into Egypt, and sold to rogue Egyptian Bedouins, and end up in torture and camps in northern Sinai.

The refugees would be tortured continuously and mercilessly to extract ransom from their impoverished families in Eritrea or in other countries.

As torture, molten plastic from burning bottles and bags would be dripped onto bare skin, causing excruciating pain. Victims were tied and left on the ground under the blazing sun. They were burned with cigarettes and electro-shock. Women were continually raped, often gang-raped, and men were raped as well. Victims were threatened with extraction of body organs.

The victims were forced to call relatives by cell phone, and they were tortured while on the phone so their relatives could hear their screams.

The torture business became more lucrative, and typical ransoms grew from a few thousand dollars to least $30,000 per person. Relatives who managed to raise the funds became impoverished for life.

When the Morsi government in Egypt fell in 2013, the Egyptian army restored its presence in northern Sinai, and the atrocities against the Eritrean refugees abated there.

We learned recently at a conference in Geneva that 7,000 Sinai torture survivors are presently in Israel.

But kidnapping, extortion and torture of Eritrean refugees continue to occur in Sudan, Libya and possibly other parts of Sinai. Still there seems to be little governmental effort in Sudan and Libya, to stop it; to the contrary, corrupt security officials often know of the traffic and torture, yet look the other way.

Tragically, many Eritrean refugees are torture survivors – from their time in Eritrea, or from the period of their flight, or both.

Thank you, Mr. Chairman, once again, for considering these observations.

ADDITIONAL INFORMATION

To the Mediterranean – Because the conditions of refugee life in Ethiopia and Sudan is so trying, the refugees there sometimes pay smugglers to take them to Libya with an objective of getting to a more sustainable life in Europe. But the smuggling often turns into trafficking, whereby the refugee becomes a victim of extortion and violent abuse. In some cases, the refugee is forced onto a thoroughly unsafe fishing boat bound across the Mediterranean in exchange for further payment, or even under threat of death if he or she doesn't board and pay. Thousands of Eritrean refugees have been sent to Europe this way, without regard to their well-being; and well over 1,000 have died at sea because of disasters resulting from gross overloading or grossly inadequate boats. The Mediterranean tragedy has been met with scorn from the dictator of Eritrea, who condemns all those who flee Eritrea as traitors.

Resettlement – The reception that Eritrean refugees receive in countries of refuge has been mixed. In the U.S., the very limited number of refugees who have been officially processed by UNHCR overseas then admitted to our country by the State Department, of course, have been treated well during the resettlement process here, through the hard work of the network of non-profit resettlement agencies that spans our country. In Israel, the far larger number of Eritreans – larger in both absolute and proportionate terms – was originally well tolerated; but as the numbers grew they came to be resented, threatened with expulsion, and often imprisoned. Now Europe, faced with vast numbers of Eritrean and other refugees arriving from the Mediterranean, is filled with confusion about how to deal with them, and in many quarters, with considerable hostility toward the refugees. In North Africa and the Middle East, the refugees are often imprisoned by the governments there, and they live with little personal security.

And as the final insult upon injury, the Eritrean regime imposes a 2% income tax on all of its expatriates; and through its secret agents, it illegally extorts the tax payments from refugees worldwide, including in the U.S.

The plight of Eritrean refugees is so dire, so complex, so little known, and in some countries so misunderstood that it shocks all normal sensibilities. The America Team, naturally, has been attempting to bring an awareness of these conditions into the light of day. Among other things, we and another

42

organization have just produced an hour-long documentary on the situation, which we expect to be released in August, 2015.

Thank you, Mr. Chairman, once again, for considering these observations. We would be boundlessly grateful if the U.S. government could help find solutions for any and all parts of the problem – from conditions within Eritrea proper to the desperation of Eritrean refugees in flight around the world.

The Flow of Flight from Eritrea

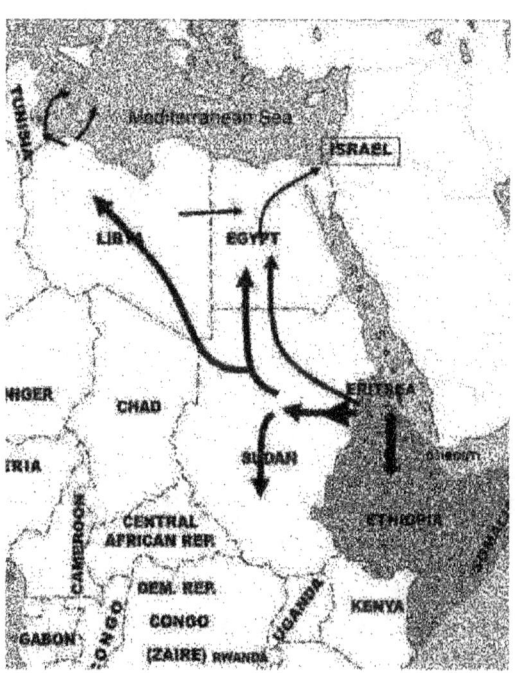

43

A torture camp in Sinai

ARTWORK FROM SINAI TORTURE SURVIVORS,
DONE WHILE JAILED IN SINAI BY EGYPTIAN POLICE

CINA SEA
CINA FIRE
CINA DESERT
CINA BAD

by Solomon
Abraha

VICTIMS OF TORTURE IN THE SINAI

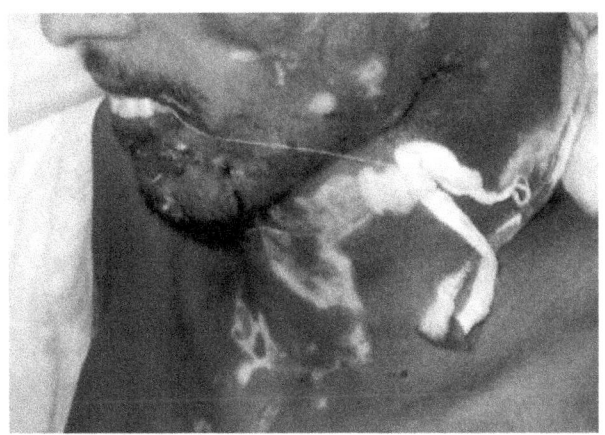

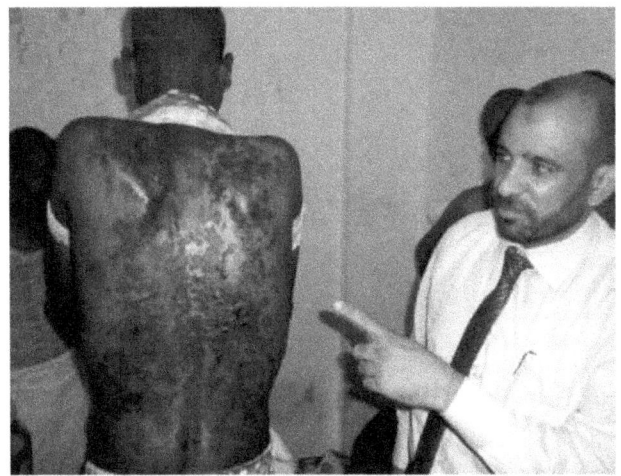

46

VICTIMS OF TORTURE IN THE SINAI

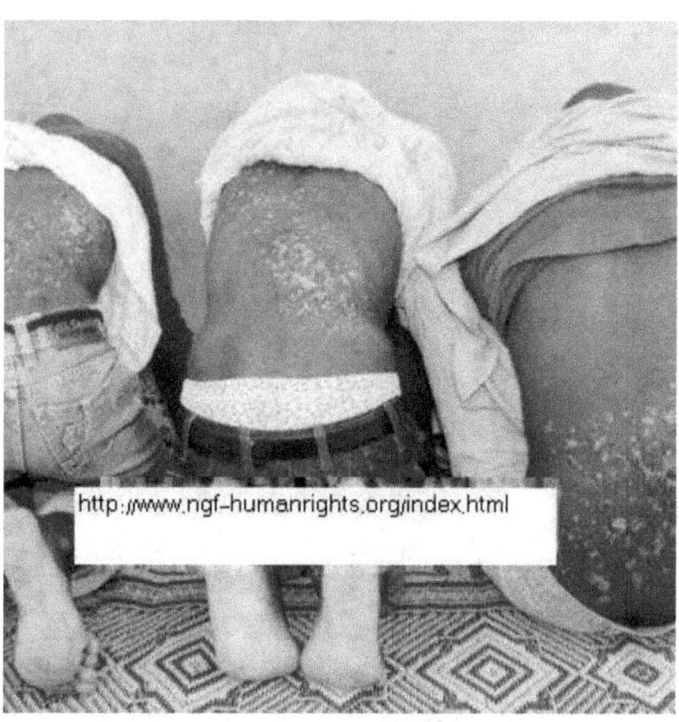

Mr. SMITH. Thank you so very much, Mr. Stauffer.
Ms. Hollingsworth?

STATEMENT OF MS. ANN HOLLINGSWORTH, SENIOR ADVO-CATE FOR GOVERNMENT RELATIONS, REFUGEES INTER-NATIONAL

Ms. HOLLINGSWORTH. Thank you.

I would like to take this opportunity to thank Chairman Smith, Ranking Member Bass, and the members of this subcommittee for holding this important hearing today.

Refugees International, or RI, is a nonprofit, nongovernmental organization that advocates for lifesaving assistance and protection for displaced people in some of the most difficult parts of the world. Based here in Washington, we conduct 12 to 15 field missions per year to research displaced populations. RI does not accept any government or United Nations funding, which allows our advocacy to be impartial and independent.

I am here today to describe the current situation for the long-standing Sudanese refugees in Chad. My colleague Michael Boyce and I went to Chad in May and June of this year, visiting the capital of N'Djamena and then to the east to meet with refugees, host communities, humanitarians, development actors, and government officials. Our new report, released today, goes into greater detail of RI's key areas of concern: Food ration cuts, as the chairman addressed earlier; and a self-reliance approach, with little funding or leadership.

Given the topic of today's hearing, I think the Sudanese refugee crisis underlines two major challenges that we see today in many parts of Africa. The first is that the most basic needs of too many vulnerable families are not being met, in large part because humanitarian funding has not kept pace with historic levels of demand worldwide. The second is that protracted displacement is not just a humanitarian problem; it is a development problem. Yet development actors are still reluctant to provide the leadership, co-ordination, and multiyear funding that could give displaced people a chance at long-term self-reliance.

The Sudanese refugee population in Chad is an underreported story, a hard thing to imagine 10 years ago when the Darfur crisis took center stage. The essential humanitarian support that both United States and the U.N. refugee agency, or UNHCR, has given to this refugee population over the years is well-documented, but there are currently 360,000 Sudanese refugees in Chad struggling to survive in a harsh environment with few opportunities available for them or for their host communities.

In early 2014, the World Food Programme, or WFP, made a dramatic 50-percent cut—up to 60 percent in some areas—in food rations for Sudanese refugees in Chad, from the previous allotment of 2,100 kilocalories a day to around 800.

We saw firsthand the effect of these cuts at a food distribution inside Am Nabak refugee camp. Both refugees and aid workers told RI that refugees, particularly women and children, had responded to the cuts with worrying coping mechanisms. Women RI spoke with left camps to find what little work they could, often farming or making bricks. Sometimes these trips would last for days or weeks at a time, with children being taken out of school to work or to care for their younger siblings while their parents were gone. An operational NGO worker that RI spoke with noted an increase in cases of sexual violence and exploitation against the Sudanese refugee women since the ration cuts began. It was clear that the consequences of food ration cuts for the most vulnerable households have been unacceptable, and an immediate increase in food assistance for these households is absolutely essential.

In the longer term, WFP and UNHCR are in the process of executing a new approach to food assistance for Sudanese refugees, one in which aid is targeted on the basis of need. The two agencies are conducting economic assessments that will divide households into four groups, from very poor to better off. Full rations would only be provided for poorer households, roughly 60 percent of all refugees, according to preliminary data. Wealthier households would receive more limited amounts of food or nonfood assistance according to their means. U.N. officials project that the transition of this approach will be completed by the end of 2015.

But, at the same time, these cuts are occurring as the humanitarian community in eastern Chad has begun to move toward a self-reliance approach for the Sudanese refugees. This approach involves giving refugees opportunities to support themselves financially, trying to strengthen ties between refugees and their Chadian neighbors, and incorporating the refugees into Chad's domestic, health, and education systems.

In principle, this transition is laudable. However, in eastern Chad, the transition faces a major and potentially fatal obstacle. The communities that refugees are meant to join are some of the poorest in the world, with extremely weak institutions, markets, and social services. In the words of one humanitarian, ''Everybody is talking about socioeconomic integration, but how do you integrate refugees into an area where people are starving?''

Humanitarian organizations like UNHCR do not have the staffing, the funding, or the mandates to fix these problems. Development donors and organizations do, yet they are virtually nonexistent in eastern Chad. That is the reality on the ground.

In refugee-hosting areas, donors and development agencies must prioritize efforts to improve water management, agricultural inputs and techniques, land management and dispute resolution, and women's empowerment.

So the way forward: Donors and the WFP must immediately increase the food rations, and I think we covered that earlier.

Secondly, donors, including USAID and the World Bank, should provide dedicated funding to development and resilience initiatives in eastern Chad that benefit both the Sudanese refugees and Chadian host communities.

And just as a sidenote, I appreciated Acting Assistant Administrator Staal recognizing the delegation visit of November trying to pull in more Middle East donor dollars. And that was great to hear, but obviously we have a long way to go.

Finally, UNHCR should freeze its budget for core refugee protection and assistance in eastern Chad. Further cuts should only be considered once refugees begin receiving long-term support from development actors.

In conclusion, I left Chad with profound stories and images of Sudanese refugees, both of despair and of strength. I listened to a female refugee who grabbed my hand to tell me about her struggles to find resources to take care of her mother and the three orphaned children in her home. I heard many stories about fears for their future, including how they will find enough food to eat. The vulnerabilities of this population are very real, and the international community must return the spotlight to them now.

Thank you very much, and I look forward to your questions.

[The prepared statement of Ms. Hollingsworth follows:]

REFUGEES INTERNATIONAL

Testimony of Ann Hollingsworth, Senior Advocate for Government Relations
Refugees International
House Committee on Foreign Affairs
Subcommittee on Africa, Global Health, Global Human Rights, and International Organizations
"Africa's Displaced People"
July 9, 2015

I would like to take this opportunity to thank Chairman Smith, Ranking Member Bass, and the members of this subcommittee for holding this important hearing today. Refugees International (RI) is a non-profit, non-governmental organization that advocates for lifesaving assistance and protection for displaced people in some of the most difficult parts of the world. Based here in Washington, we conduct 12 to 15 field missions per year to research displaced populations, most recently in locations such as South Sudan, Myanmar, Lebanon, Iraq, and Turkey. RI does not accept any government or United Nations funding, which allows our advocacy to be impartial and independent.

I am here today to describe the current situation for the longstanding Sudanese refugees in Chad. Like many of the displacement crises facing Africa today, the only real solution for the Sudanese refugees is to end the conflict and persecution that forced them to flee. But until that happens, governments and the United Nations have a duty to protect and assist these refugees to the fullest extent possible.

My colleague, Michael Boyce, and I went to Chad in May and June of 2015, visiting the capital N'Djamena and then to the east to meet with refugees, host communities, humanitarians, development actors, and government officials. Our new report, released today, goes into greater detail of RI's key areas of concern: **food ration cuts and a self-reliance approach with little funding or leadership.**

The Situation in Chad Today:

The Sudanese refugee population in Chad is an underreported story – a hard thing to imagine ten years ago, when the Darfur crisis took center stage. The essential humanitarian support that both the United States and the UN Refugee Agency (UNHCR) have given to this refugee population over the years is well-documented. But there are currently 360,000 Sudanese refugees in Chad, struggling to survive in a harsh environment with few opportunities available for them or for their host communities. Ranking 184th out of 187 countries in the United Nations Human Development Index, Chad is one of the poorest countries in the world.

The price of oil, the country's main export, has fallen roughly 40 percent since last year, and trade routes into Nigeria, Central African Republic, and Libya have been largely cut due to conflict. And regional counterterrorism efforts, particularly with respect to Boko Haram, remain a primary focus of the Chadian government. The June 15, 2015 suicide bombings in N'Djamena, which targeted both the police academy and the police headquarters, were a tragic reminder of the security threats the region is facing.

Today, new refugee flows into Chad from both the Central African Republic and Nigeria are shifting the focus of the international community away from the Sudanese refugee population. The ongoing conflict in Darfur has caused the Sudanese refugees' exile to become protracted. And though all of the refugees we spoke with want to return to Darfur, they realize that this is unlikely any time soon.

Despite appearances of being an unchanged population, the number of Sudanese refugees in Chad continues to increase. We met a female refugee named Aishe who had arrived in Chad just one week prior, having never been displaced before. When her village in Darfur was attacked by a militia, she was separated from her seven children, and had to travel for 15 days to reach the refugee camp in Chad. Aishe managed to find shelter with a sister who lives in the camp. But her family is scarcely able to support themselves, leaving her wondering how she would survive.

Given the topic of today's hearing, I think the Sudanese refugee crisis underlines two major challenges that we see today in many parts of Africa. The first is that the most basic needs of too many vulnerable families are not being met – in large part because humanitarian funding has not kept pace with historic levels of demand worldwide. The second is that protracted displacement is not just a humanitarian problem – it is a development problem. Yet development actors are still reluctant to provide the leadership, coordination, and multi-year funding that could give displaced people a chance at long-term self-reliance.

Food Ration Cuts:

In early 2014, the World Food Program (WFP) made a dramatic 50 percent cut (up to 60 percent in some areas) in food rations for Sudanese refugees in Chad: from the previous allotment of 2,100 kilocalories a day to around 800. We saw first-hand the effect of these cuts at a food distribution inside Am Nabak refugee camp. In addition to reductions in legumes, sorghum, oil, and cereals, no sugar or salt were available to the refugees. Soap happened to be part of the distribution that day but that had not been included in months, according to the refugees.

In Touloum refugee camp, we spoke with two female refugees who said it was difficult to get their children the necessary nutrition, particularly since the food rations began, as local food is expensive and items such as fruit or meat are not provided by WFP. Humanitarians that RI spoke with said women often cannot afford essentials such as milk for their children. One local NGO spoke to RI about malnourished children having to share their nutritional supplements with their families since the ration cuts began, prolonging their recovery time.

Both refugees and aid workers told RI that refugees – particularly women and children – had responded to the cuts with **worrying coping mechanisms**. Women RI spoke with left camps to find what little work they could, often farming or making bricks. Sometimes these trips would last for days or weeks at a time, with children being taken out of school either to work or care for younger siblings while their parents were gone. An operational NGO worker that RI spoke with noted an increase in cases of sexual violence and exploitation against the Sudanese refugee women since the ration cuts began. Petty crime has increased in some areas as well. It was clear to RI that the consequences of food ration cuts for the most vulnerable households have been unacceptable. An immediate increase in food assistance for those households is absolutely essential.

In the longer-term, WFP and UNHCR are in the process of executing a new approach to food assistance for the Sudanese refugees – one in which aid is targeted on the basis of need. The two agencies are conducting economic assessments that will divide households into four groups, from very poor to better off. Full rations would only be provided for poorer households – roughly 60 percent of all refugees, according to preliminary data. Wealthier households would receive more limited amounts of food or non-food assistance (such as food-for-assets and access to microcredit) according to their means. UN officials project that the transition to this new approach will be completed by the end of 2015.

Self-Reliance Approach:

It is important to note that these food rations cuts are just one example where cuts to humanitarian assistance are having an immediate impact on the refugee population. At the same time, these cuts are occurring as the humanitarian community in eastern Chad has begun to move toward a self-reliance approach for the Sudanese refugees. This self-reliance approach involves giving refugees opportunities to support themselves financially, trying to strengthen ties between refugees and their Chadian neighbors, and incorporating the refugees into Chad's domestic health and education systems.

In principle, this transition is laudable. It follows years of research suggesting that displaced people lead more dignified lives if they are self-sufficient and integrated with host communities. However, in eastern Chad this transition faces a major – and potentially fatal – obstacle: the communities that refugees are meant to join are some of the poorest in the world, with extremely weak institutions, markets, and social services. In the words of one humanitarian whom RI spoke to, "Everybody is talking about socio-economic integration...but how do you integrate refugees into an area where people are starving?"

Humanitarian organizations like UNHCR do not have the staffing, the funding, or the mandates to fix these problems. Development donors and organizations do have the mandate, yet they are virtually non-existent in eastern Chad. That is the reality on the ground.

The future for health care access is problematic. UNHCR and the Chadian authorities decided that Sudanese refugees would no longer receive healthcare at separate facilities but would instead be served through the Chadian national health system. Though a fine idea in principle, in fact health services in the east's refugee-hosting regions have been critically weakened by a lack of state healthcare workers. Aid agencies told RI that in many parts of the east, Chadian state clinics are almost entirely staffed by NGO workers paid by UNHCR and its partners. These aid agencies claim that many state-funded healthcare posts at these clinics remain vacant.

In refugee-hosting areas, donors and development agencies must prioritize efforts to improve water management, agricultural inputs and techniques, land management and dispute resolution, and women's empowerment. Many of the Sudanese refugees are skilled in agriculture and farming. To acknowledge this existing resource, development projects should focus on water management solutions.

A final priority for development donors and agencies must be women's empowerment. Sudanese refugee women and girls suffer from a low social status, with limited rights and economic power. This contributes to gender-based violence (including rape, domestic violence, and early or forced marriage), poor maternal health, and the vulnerability of women-headed households.

Immediate and Medium-Term Recommendations:

- Donors and the WFP must immediately increase food rations to 2,100 kilocalories per day for vulnerable Sudanese refugees, until such time as assistance can be adjusted in line with region-wide household economic assessments.
- UNHCR and the WFP should closely monitor the food security situation of Sudanese refugees after food assistance is adjusted. After 12 months, UNHCR and WFP should commission a full Joint Impact Evaluation to identify any necessary adjustments and to more fully understand and address coping mechanisms.
- Donors – including the United States Agency for International Development (USAID) and the World Bank – should provide dedicated funding for development and resilience initiatives in eastern Chad that benefit both Sudanese refugees and Chadian host communities.
- UNHCR should freeze its budget for core refugee protection and assistance in eastern Chad. Further cuts should only be considered once refugees begin receiving long-term support from development actors.

Conclusion:

I left Chad with profound stories and images of Sudanese refugees, both of despair and of strength. I watched elderly women in the hot sun chopping what limited firewood was available. I listened to a female refugee who grabbed my hand to tell me about her struggles to find resources to take care of her mother and the three orphan children in her home. I heard many stories about fears for their future, including how they will find enough food to eat. The vulnerabilities of this population are very real and the international community must return the spotlight to them now.

Thank you very much and I look forward to your questions.

Mr. SMITH. Ms. Hollingsworth, thank you so very much for yours.

And, Ms. Eisenbarth, if you could proceed. I am going to step out for a moment, and I apologize. I have read your testimony, so——

Ms. EISENBARTH. Great. Thank you.

Mr. SMITH. Mark Meadows will take it. There is a briefing on Srebrenica, which, again, had a resolution on the floor, but I will only be about 10 minutes. And I have a lot of questions for you folks. But my distinguished colleague can do a better job.

STATEMENT OF MS. NATALIE EISENBARTH, POLICY & ADVOCACY OFFICER, INTERNATIONAL RESCUE COMMITTEE

Ms. EISENBARTH. On behalf of my organization, the International Rescue Committee, I would like to thank Chairman Smith, Ranking Member Bass, Mr. Meadows, and members of the subcommittee for holding this hearing.

I would like to request that my written testimony be included in the record.

Mr. MEADOWS [presiding]. Without objection.

Ms. HOLLINGSWORTH. Thank you.

The International Rescue Committee, or the IRC, is a global humanitarian NGO with a presence in 22 cities in the U.S. and 40 countries worldwide, nearly half of which are in sub-Saharan Africa.

The topic of today's hearing, displacement, is at the very core of the IRC's mission. We provide emergency relief and postconflict development and help people uprooted by conflict and disaster to rebuild their lives. We share the subcommittee's deep concern about the safety and security of people who have been driven from their homes.

Displacement, whether in one's own country or across borders, leaves affected persons particularly vulnerable to economic shocks, at risk of human rights violations, without access to basic services, and often puts their physical safety in jeopardy.

The Internal Displacement Monitoring Center estimates that in 2014 in sub-Saharan Africa at least 4.5 million people were newly displaced within the boundaries of their own countries. The U.N. Refugee Agency, UNHCR, estimates that nearly 760,000 people became new refugees.

The majority of these new refugees and IDPs became displaced as a result of conflict. The circumstances of conflict-induced displacement often take years to resolve, as the subcommittee and Mr. Smith noted before. As the average length of displacement reaches 17 years, we must make a renewed commitment to help people not only survive in the midst of displacement but to regain control of their lives and thrive.

U.S. support for assistance to displaced persons typically comes through the main international humanitarian assistance accounts: The International Disaster Assistance account for IDP assistance, the Migration and Refugee Assistance, and Emergency Refugee and Migration Assistance accounts for refugees. Alongside other accounts for food assistance and support for international peacekeeping, these accounts are the backbone of U.S. support for displaced persons. Congress' support in funding these accounts is invaluable and enables the U.S. to save lives and prevent suffering.

I would like to spend the majority of my testimony devoted to what more we can do to aid those in situations of protracted displacement. When people are displaced for years on end, their needs go beyond the essential means of survival. To respond better to their needs, we must address five critical challenges common to most protracted displacement situations in Africa.

First, there must be a commitment to peace and the protection of the most vulnerable. Governments hosting refugees and experiencing internal displacement bear the primary responsibility for preserving asylum space and ensuring displaced persons receive protection and assistance.

For its part, the U.S. Government must continue to be vocal about the importance of refugee-hosting nations keeping their borders open and fostering an environment that is supportive of protecting and assisting refugees and IDPs. We also need political solutions to violent conflicts in places like South Sudan and CAR and other countries in sub-Saharan Africa. President Obama's visit to east Africa later this month is a key opportunity to reinforce such priorities.

Second, the response to displacement must be better suited to protracted situations. Assistance from the international community is often designed to provide the essentials of survival, which is challenged, as Ann noted, but saves lives. It does little to enable IDPs and refugees to thrive during what are often years away from home. The U.S. Government's funding and advocacy and support of efforts to increase self-reliance—things like supporting education for children and young people and adults' opportunities to work in local economies—their very means of self-sufficiency are essential.

Third, we must take a closer look at the traditional model of delivering assistance to displaced communities and formally recognized camps. Globally, the majority of displaced individuals do not reside in formal camps or collective sites. Instead, they are living with relatives, with friends, or securing accommodations on their own, often in urban settings. Assistance must be tailored to ensure that these refugees and IDPs do not fall through the cracks and receive the assistance they need.

In July 2014, a year ago, the UNHCR released a new policy on alternatives to camps. The policy sets a vision for UNHCR service to refugees, recognizing that while camps are an important tool, they remain long after the reasons for their existence have passed. As it stands now, the policy does not incorporate how it should apply to the IDP populations around the world, which is a critical area for attention in the future.

The U.S. Government should continue to support and enable UNHCR to align its practice with the vision in this policy and continuously adapt its own assistance to ensure it is reflective of the reality that most displaced communities reside outside camps, and it should encourage other international actors to do the same.

Fourth, we must align better international support based on need. Displaced persons are often living in underdeveloped places where the host communities alongside whom they reside are themselves quite marginalized and vulnerable. Ann mentioned this with respect to the situation in Chad. Addressing the needs of IDPs and refugees in these settings provides a unique opportunity to better integrate their service provision into efforts to assist host communities.

Ensuring that assistance is targeted to the displaced alongside host communities involves a recognition that protracted displacement is not simply a humanitarian issue but also a development problem. The World Bank now recognizes displacement as a development issue. Other development donors, including the U.S., should be encouraged to align their programming and funding accordingly.

Fifth, I mentioned the critical humanitarian accounts previously. The U.S. must continue to provide this critical foreign assistance—it is a leader in providing humanitarian assistance around the world—and, of course, continuous improvements to aid delivery to make it more effective and efficient.

I would like to close by highlighting two countries in Africa that exemplify these challenges.

First, South Sudan, a country that is today marking its fourth anniversary of independence, has been in the grip of violent conflict since December 2013. Civilians are bearing the brunt of this violence and often use displacement as a survival strategy. Protection is paramount in this case.

The U.S. Government must continue to advocate to the South Sudanese political leadership on the importance of protecting and assisting IDPs. Simultaneously, the U.S. Government must continue to support and advocate toward refugee-hosting countries on the importance of preserving asylum space while also expanding opportunities for refugees to become self-reliant.

Secondly, the Central African Republic. The IRC has been working in the CAR since 2006. In 2 weeks, we will release a new report with the intention of refocusing attention on the needs of the Central African people.

The IRC's analysis indicates that, while the international narrative on CAR is one of progress and increasing stability, humanitarian assistance is still desperately needed. However, to effectively break the cycle of violence and poverty, as is the case in many other African countries, we must take a long-term approach to addressing the challenges that create displacement while also providing the emergency assistance necessary to save lives in the short term.

I appreciate your keen attention to these issues and thank you for your time. Look forward to questions.

[The prepared statement of Ms. Eisenbarth follows:]

Written Statement for the Record

**Submitted by, Natalie Eisenbarth, Policy and Advocacy Officer,
International Rescue Committee**

**To, House Foreign Affairs Subcommittee on Africa, Global Health, Global Human Rights, and
International Organizations**

For the Hearing: "Africa's Displaced People"

July 9, 2015

The International Rescue Committee (IRC) thanks Chairman Chris Smith, Ranking Member Karen Bass, and the House Foreign Affairs Subcommittee on Africa, Global Health, Global Human Rights, and International Organizations for holding this hearing on the situation facing millions of internally displaced persons (IDPs) and refugees in sub-Saharan Africa. This hearing comes on the eve of President Barack Obama's visit to East Africa and is therefore a timely opportunity to discuss displacement in Africa in hopes of this issue figuring into the presidents' talking points and public statements.

The IRC is a global humanitarian non-governmental organization (NGO) with a presence in 40 countries worldwide and 22 cities in the United States, providing emergency relief and post-conflict development and helping refugees and people uprooted by conflict and disaster to rebuild their lives. Since its inception, the IRC has been involved in virtually every major refugee crisis and resettlement initiative around the globe. In sub-Saharan Africa, the IRC is active in 18 countries. The IRC shares the Subcommittee's deep concern about the safety and security of some of the world's most vulnerable people who have been driven from their homes.

Overview
Displacement – whether in one's own country or across borders – leaves affected persons particularly vulnerable to economic shocks, at risk of human rights violations, without access to basic services, and often puts their physical safety in jeopardy. Uprooted from jobs, schools, social networks, service providers, and the other things we all rely on for our physical and emotional well-being, internally displaced persons and refugees often rely on the care of family, friends, voluntary service organizations, and, in some cases, the international community to meet their basic needs.

Displacement can result from a number of, sometimes conflating, causes – but often they fall into one of two categories: threats to freedom and/or physical safety as a result of conflict or violence and changes in climate or other environmental shocks. The massive uptick in numbers of displaced persons from central and southern Somalia during that country's 2011 famine is an example of the epic tragedy that can result when these causes of displacement combine. Meanwhile, conflict-induced displacement is influenced by the changing nature of conflict in places like the Sahel belt. For example, in recent years, the activity of armed groups like Boko Haram and AQIM in Nigeria and Mali, respectively, have forced hundreds of thousands of people out of their homes and, for many, across borders.

The Internal Displacement Monitoring Center (IDMC) estimates that in 2014 in sub-Saharan Africa, at least 4.5 million people were newly displaced within their own countries; figures from the United Nations refugee agency (UNHCR) estimate that 759,000 became new refugees. The majority of these new refugees and IDPs became displaced as a result of conflict. Conflict-induced displacement results in tremendous trauma. And the circumstances of such displacement often take years, not weeks or months, to resolve – making the time IDPs and refugees spend away from home protracted if not permanent.

Humanitarian assistance is often delivered in sub-Saharan Africa in joint effort by UN agencies, international non-governmental organizations (NGOs), and national civil society organizations. The U.S. provides its share of assistance through several accounts: the International Disaster Assistance (IDA) account provides support for IDPs; the Migration and Refugee Assistance (MRA) and Emergency Refugee and Migration Assistance (ERMA) accounts provide support for refugees; and U.S. support for emergency food assistance primarily comes through the Food for Peace/Title II account. Congress' support in funding these accounts is invaluable and quite literally enables the U.S. to save lives and prevent immediate suffering. However, in situations of protracted displacement, people's needs go beyond the delivery of the essential means of survival – food, water, health care and protection. As the average length of displacement reaches 17 years, it is critical that we make a renewed commitment to help people not only survive but regain control of their lives and thrive.

To adequately address the needs of displaced people over the long-term, the international community, in partnership with the governments and civil society representatives in countries affected by displacement, must ensure the following:
- Commitment and resources to protect those displaced (either within their own countries or across borders) and support communities hosting them. This includes not only assistance but also a commitment to advocate for the rights of displaced, including ultimate solutions to displacement;
- Commitment to better meet the needs of those in situations of protracted displacement – both through changes in humanitarian aid delivery, diplomatic engagement with relevant government authorities, and harmonizing humanitarian and development interventions;
- Commitment to address refugee and IDP needs based on where they reside, not simply where they are easiest to reach;
- Focus on encouraging actors with leverage to find a solution to the conflicts that cause people to flee in the first place.

South Sudan and the Central African Republic unfortunately demonstrate these realities all too well.

South Sudan
In South Sudan, conflict has been raging since December 2013. Civilians have historically borne the brunt of violence and the current conflict is no different. Both government and opposition forces have committed extraordinary abuses of civilians, often deliberately targeted along ethnic lines, including mass killings, disappearances, torture and gender-based violence (GBV) such as rape. An upsurge of ethnic violence threatens to further tear the country apart.

In the midst of violence and conflict, civilians use displacement as a survival strategy. Nearly 600,000 individuals have become internally displaced since December 2013; another 1.6 million have become refugees.

In South Sudan, nearly 120,000 of those IDPs who have been displaced since fighting began are presently residing in protection of civilians (PoC) sites within or adjacent to bases of the UN peacekeeping mission in South Sudan (UNMISS). UNMISS should be commended for opening its doors to civilians under threat – U.S. funding of peacekeeping activities provides critical financial support for the mission. Civilians remain in the PoC sites largely because there has been no improvement to basic security outside the bases. They face innumerable challenges: the PoC sites themselves have not been impermeable to violence, living conditions for IDPs in many of the sites (which were not set up with the intention of hosting internally displaced people) are extremely poor, and many of the bases are extremely overcrowded.

However, the vast majority of people displaced are outside bases and formal camps: many are in remote areas and face continued threats to their security, resulting in repeated displacement. This fluid situation in rural areas has made it difficult for humanitarian agencies to reach all those in need of assistance. South Sudan – a poor and underdeveloped country which relies on assistance from the humanitarian community even in the absence of conflict – is a difficult aid delivery environment in the best of circumstances. The fighting which began in December 2013 immensely compounded these challenges, scattering communities across the country, many into remote areas with little to no access to lifesaving assistance. Donors – including USAID and its partner NGOs – and humanitarian agencies have mounted impressive efforts to ensure critical food, medicine, non-food items (NFIs), and other essential goods reached those in need. But with a recent upsurge in fighting – largely concentrated in Upper Nile State and Unity State – and no end in sight to the conflict, such gains can easily be squandered.

The IRC is working in Unity State. Like many other agencies, the IRC had to evacuate staff in April and May and are only now deploying staff back to a few critical locations. However, this region remains insecure with many communities scattering to safe havens in the bush with extremely limited communications with the outside world, no food and at risk of militias. Other displaced communities are arriving in increasing numbers to the UN peacekeeping base in the northern town of Bentiu or heading east across the Nile or north to Sudan and eventually Khartoum.

The situation for South Sudanese refugees in neighboring countries also requires urgent attention. Over half a million South Sudanese have fled their country since December 2013. Among them are extremely high numbers of female-headed households and unaccompanied and separated children (for example, 90 percent of refugees arriving in Ethiopia's Gambella region are women and children). Refugees urgently need assistance. Host countries, who are to be commended for keeping their borders open, should also be supported in seeking alternatives to refugee camps and helping refugees to become self-reliant.

Central African Republic
The IRC has been working in the Central African Republic (CAR) since 2006. Next week we will release a new report with the intention of refocusing attention on the needs of the Central African people as well as on the obstacles the IRC and other humanitarian agencies are experiencing in trying to aid the population.

The IRC's analysis indicates that while the international narrative on CAR is one of progress and increasing stability, Central Africans are very uncertain of the future of their country. Even with a reduction in violence from the peak of the recent crisis in CAR, a humanitarian catastrophe continues to unfold. Humanitarian assistance is still desperately needed and nearly 900,000 people remain internally displaced. Over 460,000 Central Africans remain refugees in neighboring Cameroon, Chad, Democratic Republic of the Congo (DRC) and Republic of Congo. While the pace of refugee arrivals in neighboring countries has decreased since mid-2014, new refugees continue to flow into neighboring countries.[1] Ongoing violence, banditry and political instability mean the conditions in CAR are largely not conducive to refugee return.

Every effort must be made to extend life-saving assistance and basic services to conflict-affected Central Africans, including to those in areas far outside Bangui. Donor governments should not turn away from humanitarian needs prematurely and should fully fund humanitarian appeals. However, to effectively break the cycle of violence and poverty, the international community must also invest in governance and security. The conclusions of the recent Bangui Forum offer the best roadmap we have to achieving this; donors must support it with funding and the diplomatic muscle to move it forward.

Ultimately, humanitarian assistance is alleviating some of the impact of the crisis on the lives of Central Africans but it is not the answer to the country's problems. As is the case in many other African countries, we must take a long-term approach to addressing the challenges that create displacement while also providing emergency assistance to save lives in the short-term.

In addition to highlighting these two case studies of current urgent needs, the IRC would like to bring attention to critical overall challenges common to most if not all humanitarian crises in Africa.

Protection

Refugees are afforded rights to protection under the international refugee convention of 1951. Individual countries have obligations under the refugee convention including the responsibility to provide asylum to persons who qualify as refugees.[2] In some cases, because of overt political expediency or implicit lack of attention to the needs of refugees, this asylum space comes under threat. The U.S. government plays a critical role, both publically and behind closed doors, in reinforcing with host country governments, the importance of preserving asylum space for refugees. For example, during his May 2015 visit to Kenya, Secretary of State John Kerry publically praised the government of Kenya in continuing to welcome refugees into Kenya and pledged additional funding to support the work of protecting and providing for refugees in Kenya.[3] In addition to support from Congress in continuing to fund the critical humanitarian assistance accounts, the U.S. government must put its diplomatic weight behind supporting refugee hosting nations to keep their borders open and foster an environment that is supportive of refugee protection. President Obama's visit to Nairobi later this month is a key opportunity to do this.

The development of legal protections for IDPs has been more recent than that of the long-standing protections afforded to refugees. Fears of intruding on country sovereignty have historically impeded

---

[1] UNHCR CAR Regional Refugee Response: http://data.unhcr.org/car/regional.php
[2] *"A person who owing to a well-founded fear of being persecuted for reasons of race, religion, nationality, membership of a particular social group or political opinion, is outside the country of his nationality and is unable or, owing to such fear, is unwilling to avail himself of the protection of that country; or who, not having a nationality and being outside the country of his former habitual residence as a result of such events, is unable or, owing to such fear, is unwilling to return to it.."* http://www.unhcr.org/3b66c2aa10.html
[3] http://www.state.gov/secretary/remarks/2015/05/241822.htm

the development of legally-binding agreements and obligations for the protection and support of persons who are displaced within the borders of their own countries. This is beginning to change with emerging consensus on the responsibilities of governments of countries with internally displaced populations. The *UN Guiding Principles on Internal Displacement*, presented to the UN Commission on Human Rights in 1998, "are based upon international humanitarian and human rights law and analogous refugee law and are intended to serve as an international standard to guide governments, international organizations and all other relevant actors in providing assistance and protection to IDPs."[4] In October 2009, governments on the African continent adopted the *Kampala Convention*. The *Kampala Convention* is the "world's first continental instrument that legally binds governments to protect the rights and wellbeing of people forced to flee their homes by conflict, violence, disasters and human rights abuses."[5] As of November 2014, 40 of the African Union's 54 member states had signed the convention and 22 had ratified it.

By ratifying and signing the *Kampala Convention*, countries commit to protect the rights of IDPs but ensuring such commitments are translated into tangible improvements in the protection of displaced populations is a long-term process that involves national policy change and implementation at all levels of government. African countries are home to nearly 12 million IDPs – more than any other continent or region. It is critical that African governments continue to establish and reinforce protections for internally displaced populations.

While UNHCR was established with a clear mandate to protect refugees, there is no equivalent intergovernmental agency to protect and assist IDPs because the country governments bear this primary responsibility. And while there are continuing improvements to the international humanitarian system's ability and capacity to support governments to meet the needs of IDPs[6], the case of South Sudan illustrates vividly why ultimately the protection of IDPs is best addressed through governments taking up their responsibility to protect and assist.

Self-sufficiency from the beginning

In addition to maintaining the commitment to support and protect refugees and IDPs in line with the rights afforded to them under international agreements, the international community, in partnership with host country governments, must ensure its response to displacement is better suited to protracted situations, which is the norm. The assistance refugees and IDPs receive from the international humanitarian community is often designed to provide the essentials of survival – basic health care, clean water, food distributions and shelter. This basic package of services saves lives but does little to enable IDPs and refugees to thrive during the months – and often years – away from home. Without access to educational opportunities and the means of providing for their families, during displacement, children and youth miss critical months and years of education and training and adults miss out on valuable opportunities to develop professional skills and contribute to the well-being of their families and communities. If self-sufficiency of refugees and displaced persons is the goal, then the international community must support and advocate for the means: children and young people's ability to attend school and attain recognized educational advancement and adults'

---

[4] http://www.brookings.edu/about/projects/idp/gp-page
[5] http://www.internal-displacement.org/assets/publications/2014/201412-af-kampala-convention-brief-en.pdf
[6] UNHCR has been encouraged to respond to situations of internal displacement in a number of UN General Assembly (UNGA) Resolutions, most notably 48/116 of December 1993, which sets out the criteria for UNHCR's engagement with internally displaced persons. While UNGA Resolution 48/116 provides the overall legal basis for UNHCR's engagement with IDPs, the Cluster approach has introduced greater predictability and accountability.

opportunity to work in local economies. Supporting such efforts to increase IDPs' and refugees' self-reliance will not only enhance their prospects during displacement but also better position them for an eventual durable solution – return home, integration into areas of displacement or, for a limited number of refugees, resettlement abroad.

One place where such an approach is working is Uganda which is hosting approximately 156,000 South Sudanese refugees who have arrived since December 2013. Uganda has a policy of promoting self-reliance for refugees. In practical terms this means the government allocates land to refugees upon their arrival in Uganda. Refugees are also able to access public services in the host community. This obviously doesn't come without challenges – particularly in an environment, like Uganda, of increasing refugee arrivals and no end in sight to the conflict in South Sudan. But the approach provides a good model for a more sustainable refugee assistance: NGOs work with government officials and local social service providers to increase capacity of public services in the area to meet the greater demand brought on by the sudden arrival of refugees. Such support also helps bolster the quality and availability of social services for members of the Ugandan host community.

Out-of-camp displacement

A critical piece of ensuring refugees receive assistance that is better suited to the protracted nature of their displacement is a closer look at the traditional default model of delivering assistance to refugee communities in the context of a formally recognized refugee camp. Globally the majority of displaced persons do not reside in formal camps or collective sites. Instead, they are living with relatives, friends or renting accommodations on their own – often (but not exclusively) in urban settings. The international community must better tailor its assistance to ensure that these refugees and IDPs are not slipping through the cracks and receive the assistance they need. Especially where people reside in non-camp settings, the ability to work becomes paramount. This is of course challenging due to host country regulations – and makes imperative investment in research on the life of refugees in local economies and advocacy with host governments to allow for arrangements to support themselves. Furthermore, one modality that has shown promise as well as impact for displaced populations is the use of unconditional cash transfers instead of non-food item (NFI) distribution and food assistance where markets and security allow. The IRC encourages the U.S. government and other donors to expand the proportion of their budgets allocated to this intervention.

In July 2014, the UN refugee agency (UNHCR) released a new *Policy on Alternatives to Camps*. The policy formally sets out a new modus operandi for UNHCR: "[pursuing] alternatives to camps, whenever possible, while ensuring that refugees are protected and assisted effectively and are able to achieve solutions". The policy recognizes that the majority of refugees live outside of formal camps and that while refugee camps are an "important tool" in responding to the needs of refugees, particularly in the first phase of an emergency, they often remain long after the "essential reasons for their existence have passed."[7]

The *Policy on Alternatives to Camps* sets an ambitious, yet sorely needed vision for UNHCR in its service to refugees. It does not incorporate how the policy should apply to the humanitarian community's response to the needs of IDPs – further revisions should include this focus with a specific emphasis on what additional challenges application of the policy to IDPs entails. The U.S. government should continue to support and enable UNHCR and its partners to align practice with the vision set forth in this policy.

---

[7] http://www.unhcr.org/5422b8f09.html

63

Need-based assistance
One opportunity to better address the needs of IDPs and refugees in situations of protracted displacement is to better tailor international support based on need, with their legal status being one, but not the only or even chief, consideration. Displaced persons often reside in under-developed places where the host communities are themselves quite marginalized and vulnerable, often resulting in tensions between the two groups. Addressing the needs of IDPs and refugees in these settings provides an opportunity to better integrate their service provision into improved social service infrastructure. Doing so by virtue better enables an extension of assistance to host communities, thereby contributing to an easing of tensions with displaced communities.

Such an approach necessarily involves a close look at how development resources are being directed to communities who are playing host to displaced persons. Often, long-term development assistance is not prioritized for the places where refugees and IDPs are residing. Ensuring that assistance is targeted to such places necessarily involves both a diplomatic and development approach – diplomacy to ensure national development plans are inclusive of both host communities and displaced persons and development to ensure assistance resources are directed accordingly.

There are examples of progress on this front. The IRC serves as co-chairs, alongside UNHCR and the UN Development Program (UNDP), an initiative called the Solutions Alliance. The U.S. government has been actively engaged in the Solutions Alliance which aims to have the displaced included in national development plans and increase their self-reliance. We are encouraged of the Solutions Alliance's progress in Somalia whereby the Peacebuilding and Statebuilding goals under the New Deal Compact now consider internally displaced and returnees to southern Somalia.

Recommendations

Protect the most vulnerable, commit to peace. Governments – those of countries hosting refugees and/or experiencing internal displacement – bear the primary responsibility for the preserving asylum space and ensuring displaced persons receive the protection and assistance to which they have a right. The U.S. government must continue to be a vocal champion of protecting and assisting refugees and IDPs – and political solutions to violent conflict in places like South Sudan and CAR. President Obama's upcoming trip to East Africa provides a critical opportunity for this.

Support refugee-hosting nations, work with partners to deliver assistance. Particularly in an environment of record-breaking displacement in sub-Saharan Africa, the U.S. government must continue to support assistance for refugees and IDPs through financial aid by supporting the critical humanitarian accounts and continuous improvements in humanitarian aid delivery. This includes expanding the use unconditional cash transfers where markets and security allow.

Ensure strong implementation of UNCHR's *Policy on Alternatives to Camps* and other efforts to deliver assistance to refugees and IDPs where they reside. Particularly in situations of protracted displacement, most displaced communities do not reside in formal camps or settlements. The U.S. government should continuously adapt its assistance to ensure it is reflective of this reality. It should encourage other international actors to do the same.

Support the development of evidence in support of advocacy on the economic and social potential of displaced communities. The U.S. government must continue to prioritize advocacy to persuade host country governments of the value of including refugees and other displaced in national development plans and to demonstrate to host communities the value of the presence of displaced communities. Such advocacy must be complemented by research to build an evidence base in support of such arguments.

Recognize that protracted displacement is not simply a humanitarian issue. Despite the humanitarian community's best efforts, until such time as the displaced are included in national development frameworks, their ability to meaningfully access services and participate in the socio-economic life of their country of residence will be limited. The World Bank now recognizes displacement as a development issue; other development donors should be encouraged to align their programming accordingly.

Mr. MEADOWS. I thank each of you for your testimony.

The chair is going to recognize the ranking member, my dear friend, Ms. Bass, for a series of questions.

Ms. BASS. Thank you, Chairman Meadows. I really appreciate that.

Ms. Eisenbarth, it might be that you hand in the testimony that you read, too, because I was trying to follow your recommendations, and I think it is different than your written testimony. So maybe you could leave us with that——

Ms. EISENBARTH. Okay. Yeah. Of course.

Ms. BASS [continuing]. You know, as well.

Well, first of all, I just want to thank the three of you for what you do—for what you do and for what your organizations do. Because it is tremendous, lifesaving work.

I wanted to ask you, Mr. Stauffer, you compared Eritrea to North Korea. And, in a way, I think one of the biggest differences is that everybody knows about North Korea; people don't know about Eritrea and what you were describing.

And, you know, I have your testimony. The people that are here don't have your testimony in front of them, but you have included in your testimony some pretty gruesome pictures about torture and torture camps. And I think that, obviously, a great deal more attention needs to be brought to the situation. I think Eritrea is very isolated, and it is not talked about a lot. So I really appreciate you bringing it forward and also, just in terms of your background, the fact that you lived there——

Mr. STAUFFER. Yes.

Ms. BASS [continuing]. That you were in the Peace Corps.

Mr. STAUFFER. Yes.

Ms. BASS. So I wanted—one, you might comment on why this is a mystery—I don't think it is just a mystery to me—but, really, why Eritrea isn't talked about, why the situation isn't highlighted there.

And then you also said that you had information about Israel that you wanted to—I wanted to give you time to do that.

Mr. STAUFFER. Well, first of all, the isolation is pretty much on purpose for the part of the regime that is in control. They don't care to invite in any outsiders that might observe what is going on or be a proponent or an agitator for democracy.

There is no oil involved in Eritrea. There actually are security issues. They have maybe 700 miles of coastline on the Red Sea. But there has been, you know—there has been some flare-ups with the press. I have worked with CNN, with Wall Street Journal, and so on, and New York Times, but it sort of just goes away then.

But this recent study by the Human Rights Council, the United Nations, is really getting people's attention. And the word is that it will be extended another year. I haven't seen that officially.

Ms. BASS. What will be? The study?

Mr. STAUFFER. The study, the COI, which basically was a team of three members who interviewed people outside the country. They were not allowed access into Eritrea. And so they interviewed people who had fled the country in many, many different places. They were here in Washington, they were in London, and they went to

Ethiopia, and so on. So this is really creating a lot of new awareness and interest.

I can also say that our organization is just about to release a 1-hour documentary on the Eritrean situation. And that will be launched at West Chester University in Pennsylvania on 8/8, August 8 at 8 p.m. So, you know——

Ms. BASS. Can you let us know—I mean, it would be—that is one thing, to do it in Pennsylvania. It would be another thing if it was known here in Washington, DC.

Mr. STAUFFER. Sure. Well, this will be the initial public screening, and, obviously, we would be delighted to—and we are planning on, you know, getting some viewership and exposure here in Washington. So we would welcome any help along those lines to make this available.

Because we are working with some networks, we cannot put it up on YouTube or Vimeo or anything like that, but we can distribute DVDs.

Ms. BASS. Well, the chairman said he would be interested in it also.

Mr. STAUFFER. Okay. Well, we will let Greg know, then, as soon as we are ready with that.

With respect to Israel, it is quite a story, actually. As I had mentioned initially around, like, 2007, Eritreans were purposely going to Israel. They were paying people to take them, drop them at the border, and they would go in and say this will be a nice life.

And, for a period of a couple of years, it went well, and they were fairly well accepted, but then the numbers increased and increased. And then, of course, the bad guys got involved, with the torture and so forth, and were dropping people at the border after they finished and got their money.

And so——

Ms. BASS. They were dropping torture victims?

Mr. STAUFFER. Yes. Yes. If a victim was tortured and then paid— and this is a whole other story. How do you pay $30,000——

Ms. BASS. Right.

Mr. STAUFFER [continuing]. And this is a network where funds— the way it would work is that the refugee was handed a cell phone. ''Call your relative, and give the relative this phone number. And we want $30,000 from you, okay? So when your relative has the money, they need to call this number, and then they will get another number, and you will find a place where you can send the money. And don't try any funny stuff or the guy in the camp is going to be killed.''

So then the money would be sent. Most of the money went to Israel, some went to Eritrea, some went to Sudan, some in the United States, some was processed through Washington. And it is unclear where all of the money was going, but there was a lot of it. And we are afraid that a lot of it was going to fund terrorism. As you may know, Eritrea is a state sponsor of terrorism, and we know that they have trained Somali individuals who are bent on terrorism.

So, anyhow, once they paid, they would be dropped at the border with Israel. If they didn't pay, they would either be forced to continue to do slave labor in the camps or they would be killed, or a lot of people were saying—and I have some evidence here—that there were organs removed from the individuals, which was fatal.

So, anyhow, the numbers in Israel began to grow and grow, and Israel never was wanting to accept them as true refugees and to assimilate at all into the society. So Israel banned UNHCR from doing RSD——

Ms. BASS. What is RSD?

Mr. STAUFFER. It is refugee status determination.

And they said, "Well, we will do it," Israel will do it. So the numbers continued to accumulate. So the peak population in Israel was about 50,000 refugees. Thirty-five thousand were Eritreans, and the balance, most of them were Sudanese and some South Sudanese.

So UNHCR had a presence there, but they weren't allowed to do RSD.

And then, finally, in 2012 into 2013, they built a wall, a fence, along the border with Egypt, so the influx stopped. The refugees are—they jailed a lot of them with public statements saying that we are going to make their lives miserable so that they will want to go back to their own country. So about 5,000 of the Eritreans have now left Israel, one way or another. Some of them have ended up in Libya and at the hands of ISIS.

And they have built a big prison toward the south end of Israel, where a lot of them are being kept. It is a horrific story.

They are gradually starting to do some RSD in Israel. We provided a Tigrigna, Eritrean language, translation of the Israeli RSD form to help the individuals. So at least they are going on record that they have applied for it.

Ms. BASS. Given that the situation is so isolated, is it possible that they are not aware of the torture and what is going on?

Mr. STAUFFER. Frankly, this is one of the drivers for our documentary, and——

Ms. BASS. What is? The——

Mr. STAUFFER. What you are saying.

Ms. BASS [continuing]. Torture?

Mr. STAUFFER. So, for awareness in Israel——

Ms. BASS. Oh.

Mr. STAUFFER [continuing]. That we will make a Hebrew version of this with Hebrew subtitles, which will document the fact—because this is it. I mean, this is a statement that—are you really a refugee, or are you an economic migrant just coming in?

Ms. BASS. Right.

Mr. STAUFFER. And they call them infiltrators, you know. They don't call them refugees.

So the number of Eritreans in Israel now is about 30,000. And, as I mentioned, 7,000 of them are torture survivors.

Ms. BASS. And when you say that the 30,000—they are not in prison? They are in the general population?

Mr. STAUFFER. Some of them are in prison. If I had to estimate, there are probably around 5,000 in prison. The rest are in the south, the southern part of Tel Aviv. That is where the bulk of them—they are also scattered around in the country, but most of them, they congregate in Levinsky Park in Tel Aviv.

And the whole issue of whether they can work is they get these temporary visas, and then the employers can get in trouble, though, if the person doesn't have a visa. And there are no real public health benefits available to these folks.

Ms. BASS. Is there any international observation of the conditions in the prison? You say there is no public health—there is no health—I mean, there has to be.

Mr. STAUFFER. I am not aware that there is. There are a couple of people from the Hotline for Refugees and Migrants who are allowed access to the prisons.

I don't know that the conditions in the prisons are all that bad compared to other places, but the point is that they are in prison. And, you know, they haven't really done anything wrong, other than cross into the country. You know, these are not lawbreakers otherwise. I mean, the Israelis would say they are lawbreakers for being illegal aliens, but other than that, no.

Ms. BASS. Thank you.

Just one final question. Ms. Hollingsworth, you described refugees being divided by their income, and you said some were better off and wealthier. And I just wonder, what does that mean to somebody who is in an IDP camp?

Ms. HOLLINGSWORTH. Thank you for the question.

Yes, this household economic assessment, I think, done by World Food Programme and UNHCR is a strategy to be more strategic with its assistance. And, again, I think that is a laudable effort.

So I think the strategy here is to look at those who are truly the most vulnerable to be able to actually get more assistance to them than they are receiving today and lessening the kind of assistance for those that—I wouldn't use the term ''wealthy,'' but better off in the terms of at least having a few more resources available.

And we saw this, as an example, in one of the refugee camps. We spoke with many refugees during our visit, and it was described to us how much the vulnerable refugees were leaning on the other refugees that maybe had a little bit more to share. Now, again, I want to be clear, that is a very small percentage.

Ms. BASS. Thank you very much.

And thank you, Mr. Chairman, again.

Mr. SMITH [presiding]. Thank you.

Mr. Meadows?

Mr. MEADOWS. Thank you, Mr. Chairman.

Mr. Stauffer, if you get your video done in Hebrew, I will give you my personal assurance that we will get as many copies as you can provide to the appropriate people in Israel at the very highest levels of government to make sure that they are aware of it.

I think for the vast majority of Americans, the overwhelming majority of Americans, one, they don't even know that this country exists, let alone the unbelievable, horrific things that you are describing. And the U.S. population, by and large, is a very kind and benevolent; when they see a need, they will reach out. We have seen that over and over and over again. And yet this particular issue is not one that has been highlighted.

So, as it relates to both here in the United States, I know the chairman and ranking member are very committed to making sure that that message gets out, but you have my personal assurances that from an Israeli perspective I will be glad to make sure that the appropriate people get that.

To give you a perspective, they have a hospital right below the Golan Heights that serves Syrian people that come across, and yet the Syrians can't even tell them that they have been served in Israel, for fear of retaliation when they return.

And so I would like to believe that this is a matter of information and not just turning a blind eye. So we will work on that.

Mr. STAUFFER. Thank you.

Mr. MEADOWS. Let me come to you. One of the issues that you talk about at the very end of your testimony is a long-term development plan. And for many Americans, that is a real concern. When you say long-term development or any foreign aid—you know, I share many times that I am big on foreign aid. It does not get me votes back home in North Carolina. It is not a positive thing.

So, with that, how do we target that development aid, where we are not in a jobs program or we are in an education program, where we are meeting the very basic humanitarian needs and yet not in what some people would call nation-building?

Ms. EISENBARTH. Right. So thank you for that question.

I agree, from your earlier remark, that the American people are quite benevolent. I also understand some of the challenges with selling foreign aid back to your constituencies at home.

First, I would say that foreign assistance on the humanitarian side primarily is my focus. But on the development side, there have been some very strong accomplishments in terms of making a difference on eliminating child mortality, improving water and sanitation, improving access to health care, including access to antiretroviral drugs, prevention of HIV. All of these things are strong successes.

Mr. MEADOWS. So when you are talking about that as development, see, many of us would put that more on the humanitarian side of it, because, you know, it gets back to what Ms. Hollingsworth was talking about, some are considered well-off versus not well-off.

Ms. EISENBARTH. Right.

Mr. MEADOWS. Well, even the well-off folks that we are talking about, their annual income is what even the poorest of the poor here would—they would be appalled at what wealthy——

Ms. EISENBARTH. Right.

Mr. MEADOWS [continuing]. Is in some of these nations.

Ms. EISENBARTH. Yeah. So, when we are talking about development, I would like to think of it as creating efficiencies in the humanitarian system, I think both from the perspective of eliminating, if we can, or at least addressing the causes of displacement.

So when you have populations, for example, in eastern DRC who are continuously facing displacement because of violence, because of lack of development there, that we are not just continually meeting basic needs but looking at the long-term causes of the vulnerability of those populations. And so, instead of just feeding—the adage of giving a man a fish but then giving a man a fishing pole.

And so looking at what we can do—of course not creating a jobs program, but looking at what we can do to help populations become more self-sufficient, particularly from the perspective of communities that are facing displacement, that are facing marginalization by the countries where they are residing, both the host communities that are hosting displaced populations but also the people that are displaced there.

Mr. MEADOWS. All right.

And so how do we address the difference between the political aspect of this conflict—because many times it is political, but oftentimes it is also tribal. And so, when we look at it specifically within Africa, you look at a different people group. You know, having spent a lot of time and being familiar with what is now South Sudan, spending time on the ground in Kenya, it is not always necessarily a political conflict, as we see in some of the ones that you are talking about. It has bigger underlying issues with regards of just whether there is peace in the region. And so we can go in and we can supply the development side of things, and yet that gets overrun by a different people group.

So how do we best do that? And/or—and I will give you maybe an easier place here—what is the role of U.N. peacekeepers as it relates to that?

Ms. EISENBARTH. So the first question about the role of the political side, perhaps, of the U.S. Government and the political dynamics underlying conflict, I would say that it is not an either/or scenario—people are facing some severe circumstances overseas, as you have mentioned, particularly those who are in the midst of the crossfire, in the midst of conflict. And so you need to provide humanitarian assistance to meet immediate needs. You also need a longer-term approach to help those communities become self-sufficient. But you also need—the U.S. has a lot of leverage, in some places more than others, to persuade parties to the conflict to make peace, to get over their political differences.

I think in the case of South Sudan and other places, CAR being one of them—from what I know of those conflicts, it is not necessarily at its core a tribal or an ethnic conflict.

Mr. MEADOWS. Right.

Ms. EISENBARTH. It is, rather, those kinds of identities being exploited, if I may, by parties to the conflict to gain popular support for their armed movement, in many cases. And so you have to have the, like I said, I think there is a lot that can be done on the political side, using the U.S. leverage, to persuade parties to the conflict to make peace.

And I forgot your second question.

Mr. MEADOWS. U.N. peacekeeping.

Ms. EISENBARTH. Oh, U.N. peacekeeping. Thank you.

It is, obviously, a quite complex role that the U.N. peacekeepers are playing. It is in constant need——

Mr. MEADOWS. It is interesting that you say that, because I don't see it as that complex. I think maybe the definition of where we need to go with U.N. peacekeeping and how it is defined perhaps needs to be redefined. Because what we have done is we have had a certain model there.

But we will follow up on that.

Ms. EISENBARTH. Okay.

Mr. MEADOWS. And, Ms. Hollingsworth, did you want to comment——

Ms. EISENBARTH. Can I just say one last thing, though?

Sorry, Ann.

I think it is in need of constant evolution and looking at how to improve the system, but it does save lives. For example, in South Sudan, you have now, as of Tuesday, the U.N. was reporting 150,000 people in U.N. peacekeeping bases. And so I will be the first to admit that it is challenged and it needs improvements, but it does save lives and is a worthwhile investment.

Ms. HOLLINGSWORTH. Thank you. So, just circling back on development, I actually think Chad is a great example here to be referencing, because when we look at what Deputy Assistant Secretary Wiesner raised in her comments today; Chad actually wants the refugee population to be integrated. And so they have made small steps to incorporate the refugees into both the education and healthcare systems.

Now, from what we heard and from what we saw on the ground, the capacity is definitely not there, but there are discussions about the national development plan. There are a lot of things being discussed right now in Chad. And Chad could be great case study, because when we look at, sort of, the political angle to this and what the role the host countries should be taking, we have a couple of specific recommendations for Chad within our report specifically targeted at that.

Secondly, on your peacekeeping question, we haven't brought up what is going on in Darfur right now, and I wanted to briefly raise this, just with the UNAMID context, very briefly. Now, this is in no way a perfect peacekeeping mission, but I just want to circle it back to what we saw on the ground in eastern Chad, which is along the Sudan border. This situation is fluid, and the violence in Darfur is increasing.

The Sudanese refugee population in eastern Chad, while it is viewed as being quite chronic—and most of the refugees we spoke with had been there for 10 to 12 years—we did meet a refugee who had fled 6 days prior and had never been a refugee before. So, basically, a militia group had said they were going to do an attack on her village. It took her 15 days to get to the refugee camp inside Chad, where her sister was. Her family was scattered. She had no idea how she was going to survive and take care of herself.

This ties back to UNAMID, which is the importance of the protection of civilian capacity that we are looking at right now. And access for humanitarian actors has been a longtime problem in Darfur. But I did want to note that Darfur definitely has fallen a bit off the radar, and the increased violence that is going on in there needs to be addressed. And UNAMID really needs to be there right now.

Thanks.

Mr. MEADOWS. All right. Thank you.

I will close with this last question. And, I guess, if you can keep it as brief as possible, because we have some better questions to follow.

With U.S. involvement in all of these different areas, how do we avoid the image of coming in and trying to set up our own governments, whether they be public governments or ones that are controlled by the United States?

Because there is a big pushback with that, they want the humanitarian aspect of it but not necessarily the conflict resolution aspect of this.

So how do we do that most effectively? And can you point to any examples where that has worked well, where the host country has said, we appreciate you coming in? It has been that fine balance of support but yet not so much of control.

Ms. EISENBARTH. So I think both Ann and I have referenced, in terms of restructuring development so that it does become more tailored to the needs of displaced populations and better linked with humanitarian aid efforts, we both have referenced the need to, through perhaps behind-the-scenes diplomacy, using the leverage that I mentioned earlier that the U.S. has, getting behind a national development plan, so that it is not the U.S. coming in and pushing its way onto the development agenda of host-country governments but, rather, getting behind them using, perhaps, evidence.

There is a growing body of work that supports the importance of using development to address protracted displacement crises but working in partnership with host-country governments and their own development plans instead of bringing in our own agenda. I think that is one example.

It is happening in Kenya.

Mr. MEADOWS. Right.

Ms. EISENBARTH. There is a lot of opportunity there with the devolution process to really partner with the Kenyans. And, obviously, Kenya is one of the leading refugee-hosting countries.

Mr. MEADOWS. Right. All right.

Ms. Hollingsworth?

Ms. HOLLINGSWORTH. I will be brief: Consultation, consultation, consultation.

In the example of Chad, I think it is important to note that the U.N. Security Council endorsed a U.N. Integrated Strategy for the Sahel. So I think that is a good angle, as well, when we talk about the neighbors being involved with what we want for the individual country so, again, it is not just the U.N. Government coming in.

Thanks.

Mr. STAUFFER. My experience, of course, is really focused on Eritrea. And I think, there is no prescription other than trying to continue to work on a humanitarian basis and diplomatically and have dialogue to see if there is any path forward that will change the behavior of the regime.

But the knee-jerk reaction there has always been that you are trying to put us down, you are trying to keep us from being successful, you are trying to support Ethiopia, our enemy, and so forth.

So I would really leave this to the diplomats to figure out if there is a way, but I think, not pushing for democracy but rather pushing for improvements in humanitarian behavior.

Mr. MEADOWS. All right.

Mr. Chairman, thank you so much.

I apologize to each of you. I have to pop out. But we are monitoring this back in my office. But thank you so much for your leadership.

Mr. SMITH. Thank you very much, Mr. Meadows.

Thank you for your testimonies and your leadership.

Just a couple of questions, first to Mr. Stauffer.

As you know, Eritrea is a Tier 3 country in our TIP Report designations—in other words, an egregious violator. In your testimony, you have elaborated much more than the TIP Report did in terms of the horrific nature of this ransom, of this scheme, $30,000 per person, the torture business, as you pointed out.

My question is, in 1998, I wrote a law called the Torture Victims Relief Act. It has been reauthorized four times, and I have a pending bill now to reauthorize it once again.

There are torture centers, victims centers all over the world. We give money to the U.N. Voluntary Fund for Victims of Torture for their centers, as well.

You mentioned 7,000 Sinai torture victims currently in Israel. I am not sure how many are here and whether or not they are getting the post-traumatic stress help that they so desperately need that these centers can provide in a very unique way. If you could speak to that?

Mr. STAUFFER. My understanding is that there is none of this going on for these 7,000 in Israel. And that was a topic of discussion with the NGO, the Hotline last week, was about how to get mental health attention to these folks in Israel.

There is the Center for Victims of Torture affiliate in Ethiopia that is helping at camps in Tigray, which is in northern Ethiopia.

But a lot of them, I am sure, in the United States, for example. You know, the U.S. brings in Eritrean refugees and resettles them officially. And many of these are torture survivors, and they don't really talk about it. They don't want to talk about it; they don't want to reveal it. So I think there are a lot that are going untreated, and it is a shame. But, you know, if it is an Eritrean, they should be screened for torture. That is all I can say.

Mr. SMITH. I deeply appreciate you bringing that to my attention and to our attention as a subcommittee. Again, I wrote that law, and I did not know they weren't getting help either in Israel, and I don't know about getting it here.

You know, some of the estimates put it at as many as 500,000 of our asylees in the United States were torture victims, some to different degrees of course. And the terrible abuse that you cited in your testimony——

Mr. STAUFFER. Yeah. I serve as——

Mr. SMITH [continuing]. Certainly has traumatic PTSD——

Mr. STAUFFER [continuing]. A witness in asylum cases in the United States, and I see these declarations month-in and month-out. And exactly. That is why they are asylees. That is why they have gone to the trouble of going to Central America and going to country to country to country into Texas, because of this mistreatment.

Mr. SMITH. And they do need to be encouraged to get the help.

Mr. STAUFFER. Yes.

Mr. SMITH. Because it is so deeply repressed. I mean, we have held hearings and heard from victims who got not total relief but a great deal of relief from the burdens, the sleepless nights, the chemical dependencies that follow because they just can't cope with what they have been through.

So I would love to work with you on trying to ensure that our Government is doing—and we will contact the Israelis, as well—make sure that at our centers, at least, there is an outreach to the Eritrean community to ensure that they get that help.

Mr. STAUFFER. Okay. Great. Thank you.

Mr. SMITH. We are looking to mark up our reauthorization very shortly. So, you know, thank you for bringing all of this to my attention and to the subcommittee's attention.

Eritrea signed the torture convention in September 24, 2014. And I am wondering what tangible impact that has had with regards to the panel of experts that oversee the torture convention at the United Nations. Have they looked into torture by the government or its complicity in torture?

Mr. STAUFFER. Not that I am aware of. I am not sure how they would look into it other than what has already been done with people that have left the country. I mean, you—there is no access, no ability to do any forensic studies within the country.

Mr. SMITH. Because very often, you know, a Special Rapporteur can go and visit, do a study, doesn't have——

Mr. STAUFFER. The Special Rapporteur is not allowed in the country.

Mr. SMITH. Okay. If I could, Ms. Hollingsworth, you heard the exchange earlier with the panel for the administration and again, the subcommittee appreciates you bringing to our attention just, as you pointed out, humanitarian organizations like UNHCR do not have staffing, funding or mandates to fix these problems, talking about Chad and the 360,000 refugees from Darfur that are there, and please let us know how we could be even more helpful as we go through the appropriations cycle and trying to ensure that our response—I remember traveling with Ambassador Williamson, and Greg and I have been to Darfur, we have been to camps so—in Darfur. We actually met with Bashir and argued with him in Khartoum. It was not a pleasant time.

But that said, I was with Ambassador Williamson at the U.N. Human Rights Commission, when it was still a commission, not a council, and the reluctance to call what was going on in Darfur a genocide was appalling. They just didn't want to call it that, and if we have taken our eye off the ball prematurely, which we may have with regards to Darfur, I think your timely reminder as well as with the refugees' situation is a very important one. If you wanted to elaborate on that at all, please do.

And then the issue that you raised so well about the food rationing cuts, that needs an immediate response. Malnutrition and the undersupply of these important food stuffs, we have got to address that. So maybe you could elaborate on that if you would.

Ms. HOLLINGSWORTH. Thank you, Mr. Chairman. First, I would say that as much as we can during the appropriations process, the development assistance is incredibly important through the lens, as I have stated, through Chad. When I talk specifically about how UNHCR does not have the funding or resources, I think the technical expertise is also an important part of this, and particularly when we look at those actors who are able to commit long term to projects on water, which is so essential to Chad, that is really the angle that we view as one of the most essential, as far as development projects.

Secondly, to the food rations, again, I really appreciate you pushing this with the first panel. We also want to be very clear that this is to fill a gap that we saw on the ground. We are not saying that the restoration of the 2,100 calories will be forever. This is more until the household economic assessments can be done and the new assistance strategy can be implemented. And most importantly, Mr. Chairman, once that is implemented UNHCR and others need to very tightly monitor the coping mechanisms and impact on what is happening to the population, and to be able to fix that as this moves forward. Thank you.

Mr. SMITH. Can I ask you, are you satisfied that anti-human trafficking efforts for the IDPs and the refugees are as robust as they could be?

Ms. HOLLINGSWORTH. We didn't look into that. So I can't address that today.

Mr. SMITH. Thank you.

Ms. Eisenbarth, in your testimony about the Central African Republic, again, all of it was excellent, but just to ask you a question with regards to that, 900,000 IDPs, 460,000 refugees, and you cite obstacles that the IRC and other humanitarian agencies are experiencing. Could you elaborate on what those obstacles are?

Ms. EISENBARTH. Yeah. So as I noted in my testimony, I think we are in a better place, overall, in CAR, but I want to underscore that we shouldn't just see the country as on the road to progress, that there are still a number of obstacles, and I think primarily the one that we are experiencing is addressing humanitarian needs outside the capital. The country is still in the grip of some pretty serious insecurity, and it is very difficult for humanitarian actors, the IRC, others, to access populations that are outside some of the main population centers. Bangui, of course, being one of them, but other major towns upcountry, and so that continues to be a challenge that befuddles our ability to get access to the populations that need humanitarian assistance that have essentially no access to basic services.

Mr. SMITH. As you point out in your testimony, the average length of displacement reaches 17 years. Is that African centric, or is that an average——

Ms. EISENBARTH. I think it is a global figure, yeah, yeah.

Mr. SMITH. Global figure. Okay. Is it worse——

Ms. EISENBARTH. It might be, but I can't say specifically, but I think it is definitely indicative of Africa, perhaps, if not worse.

Mr. SMITH. Just let me ask, finally, if I could of you, Mr. Stauffer, what has the ICC done vis-à-vis Eritrea? You know, we know that they have been slow, but they are looking at indictments of a couple of Boko Haram people. They have had one conviction of a DR Congo person who committed genocide, but it seems to me that the ICC could be doing more, particularly with a country that has been so barbaric. You called it the North Korea of Africa. And what has the AU done vis-à-vis Eritrea to really bring focus and attention——

Mr. STAUFFER. Well, I am not aware of anything that the ICC has done. Certainly there has been a lot of effort in Europe to raise awareness about as much—the situation in Eritrea it is much more aware in Europe than it is here, partly because of the many Eritreans that have come across the Mediterranean, but—and there has been some really strong advocacy by several folks, several Eritrean folks in Europe to create awareness, but, you know, whether the ICC has even taken any, you know, action or whatever internally, I just don't know.

And as far as the AU, there has been a process, a thing called the Khartoum process where they are attempting to work through—mainly diplomatically and maybe some economic aspects to stop the flow of people coming out of Sudan, out of Eritrea, moving up to the Mediterranean and so on. But there is, frankly, I think, it has been lip service that has been coming from Eritrea that they are going to try to stop the departures and so forth.

And just as a thing that is really gotten things stirred up is that the Danes sent in a team into Asmara to try to figure out, we are giving all this asylum to Eritreans. Should we really be doing it or are things as bad as they—and they came out with a report that: Oh, things are getting better and they are working hard on it. They should know that going to Asmara is the last place in the world they will get the answer to this type of question. And they did not get any corroboration for anything good happening when they went south in Ethiopia and talking to other people.

And, unfortunately, the Brits have been trying to utilize this flawed report that, you know, things aren't at bad as they supposedly are in Eritrea. But all indications are that it is business as usual, and there has been nothing substantial to change things, ICC or otherwise.

Mr. SMITH. Has the Atrocity Prevention Board acted in an early warning prevention capacity? Has it worked? Ms. Eisenbarth?

Ms. EISENBARTH. I, to be on honest, have not followed their work closely. But my organization has been, of course, watching the situation in Burundi. We were active in Burundi long before the current crisis, and of course, are now responding both on the Burundi side and the Tanzania side. From my understanding, there was a lot of work done by the Atrocity Prevention Board to draw attention to the crisis in Burundi. And so, I think it did catalyze some attention. Whether or not it could have done more to prevent where we are now with the country, that is my most recent experience with the APB, and so that is the best I can say.

Mr. SMITH. I had asked the previous panel, and maybe you might want to respond to it on the first 1,000 days from conception to the second birthday. Have you found in IDP settings and refugee protection settings that there is an awareness that, again, if you get that from conception that first month, second month, third month, if you get that right, that child's life is exponentially enhanced on a myriad of fronts. If you don't, it is lost. You don't turn stunting around when they are 2. So I am wondering, you know, if you have seen an awareness of that? The first amendment I offered that became law here in the early 1980s with the Child Survival Fund, a $50 million authorization, and I traveled to El Salvador during a day of tranquility between from FMLN and the Duarte government to see that money used to vaccinate kids against pertussis, diptheria, polio, and the like.

And so I am a big fan of vaccinations. Every dollar spent there is transformational as well, and it is right in line with this idea of early intervention having a huge impact. And I am wondering if you have seen in the first 1,000 days are kids getting their vaccinations as toddlers and as young children, neonates, even, in these camps? Is that——

Ms. EISENBARTH. I appreciate your attention to this. I have a personal passion for this issue as well. So I appreciate the question. The IRC is quite active in malnutrition programming in many of the countries where we are working. One program that has proven quite effective in terms of delivering first-line treatment and identification of symptoms of some of the leading causes of child mortality has been the Community Case Management Program in South Sudan. I will have to get back to you with the exact figure, but it has resulted in somewhere on order of 80-percent reduction in child mortality by addressing some of these leading killers of children early on.

The IRC is currently doing some research into how we might integrate malnutrition identification and first-line treatment into this program. I think particularly in an area like South Sudan, it is quite difficult to access, and I think it applies to other countries as well, but in South Sudan, it is quite difficult for families to reach health clinics, for even humanitarian actors to set up operations, formal operations, near where communities are displaced. Having a program like the Community Case Management Program, where you have community caseworkers going into communities, sometimes, in large part, on foot, to work with communities to address some of these leading causes of child mortality is very effective.

And, again, we are looking to see how we might integrate malnutrition into that. The IRC actually released a report on malnutrition in South Sudan just 2 months ago, and I think it is important, from our perspective, to look at some of the ways like this modification to this program where we can improve the humanitarian response, but particularly in a case like South Sudan, the conflict there has really set back efforts to address some of the underlying causes of children not being able to be well-nourished in their first 1,000 days, for mothers as well. And it underscores the importance of finding a political solution to this conflict, so that we can get the communities in South Sudan back on the path to development to address issues like access to safe water, access to health clinics, all of these—access to food, all of these different drivers of malnutrition. So I can send that report to your staff.

Ms. HOLLINGSWORTH. Thank you. I did want to take note that once the food ration cuts began in 2014, UNHCR did do a nutrition survey to look at the impact, and our understanding is the takeaways from the results of that survey was the malnutrition rates had basically stayed about the same. We saw a little bit of a different opinion when we spoke to the refugees themselves, particularly the women spoke about the children, and obviously the food concerns of access to food was something that was raised time and again. I will say that something we raised in the report is particularly important for what you raise, Mr. Chairman, is the nutritional supplements which have continued, and that has been our understanding. The problem is that the children that are receiving those nutritional supplements are sharing those with their extended family because the food rations have overall been cut. So because they are sharing, it means the recovery for their malnutrition takes much longer. So I think that is an important context when we look at the underlying concerns around this. Thank you.

Mr. SMITH. About 15 years ago, Greg Simpkins and I were in Lagos, and were speaking on human trafficking protection of unborn children, which I am very pro-life. I believe in womb-to-tomb protection. And a man came up to me and says: Well, what are you doing about autism in Nigeria? And I said: Nothing. Doing a lot in my own country. I have no idea you have a big problem here. Again, I asked the previous panel about this, and we have been working with his NGO ever since. His wife is a medical doctor in Lagos. He works for Exxon. And there is such an unmet need in Africa. WHO says tens of millions of children are on the spectrum. We had a woman from Cote d'Ivoire testify at one of our hearings on a global brain health bill that deals well Alzheimer's, autism, and hydrocephalic condition, which is also devastating in Africa, and she said there was nothing whatsoever for my child. She now is in Ohio and has gotten services which have helped her son. So I have been raising it everywhere I go, and I am wondering, again, twice jeopardize a child who is in a refugee camp or an IDP camp who is on the spectrum may not even be recognized for what he or she is suffering, and I am wondering if you have seen any evidence of an awareness of a need to address autism in that setting, because they are there?

Ms. EISENBARTH. I can't speak to a global awareness of autism. I just will say that there is an awareness on the critical importance of women, women who are of childbearing age, women who are already pregnant, or who are likely to conceive of also being the beneficiaries of nutrition programs. There have been a number of efforts in refugee settings to innovate and try to tailor specialized feeding programs for women. But in terms of sort of rooting that in an awareness of autism, I can't speak to that.

Mr. SMITH. Is this something you could just keep in mind as you go forward?

Ms. EISENBARTH. Of course. I will flag it for country teams.

Ms. HOLLINGSWORTH. I can't speak to the autism issue, but just to support Natalie there on the issue of women's health issues and concerns, one thing I did want to flag that I haven't had the opportunity to is the issue of—I raised in my testimony women leaving camps to find jobs and other things. The issue of getting water is particularly important, and one of the female refugees we spoke with talked about the daily trek to go find water outside the refugee camp. And unfortunately, much of that water is contaminated.

So what would happen was she would bring the water back, she would get sick, her children would get sick, her neighbors would get sick. So this is a healthcare issue that I am sure you know quite well, but I think it is important in this context to raise with this opportunity. So thank you.

Mr. SMITH. No. Thank you. Thank you for underscoring.

One final question, and it is on DR Congo. Can you shed any light on that refugee and IDP situation? Again, Greg and I were there in Goma. It has been a while. And we do have a distinguished Member of the Congress, of the House, with us today who deals with that issue as well. If you could, yes, Ms. Eisenbarth.

Ms. EISENBARTH. I think eastern DRC is actually a perfect case study for some of the issues that I have raised in my testimony. As I said previously, I don't know if you were in the room, Mr. Smith, but many communities in eastern DRC are facing repeated displacement. Often remaining displaced for years on end, and it is important to really look at the holistic needs of those communities, that we are not just delivering assistance along the peaks and valleys or the conflict crisis situation in eastern DRC, but really taking a long-term approach to addressing needs there.

We were thankful to see the appointment of Mr. Perriello as the new special envoy for the Great Lakes region because, again, looking at some of the underlying drivers of displacement and some of the political issues that have been persisting in eastern DRC and the region for many years is essential to providing the stability that communities need to meet their needs and to thrive.

Ms. HOLLINGSWORTH. Thank you for mentioning the Democratic Republic of the Congo. RI has produced three reports over the past 12 months. Most recently, it was on looking specifically at the USAID programs, 5-year holistic programming for gender-based violence, and that was released. For the purposes of this hearing, though, I would like to raise the concerns around refugee support versus IDP support in the DRC, and I think the refugees themselves inside the DRC are receiving assistance. It is those 2.7 million or so IDPs that are, quite frankly, neglected at this point. We have been championing this for several months to get more assistance directly to them, and we hope you will raise this as well. So thank you.

Mr. SMITH. So thank you very much for your leadership. As you come up with ideas that you think we could help amplify or need to work on, please let us know. We do have a hearing on Burundi scheduled for the July 22, and we really hope to bring some additional focus on that crisis as well.

Thank you again. The hearing is adjourned.

[Whereupon, at 4:30 p.m., the subcommittee was adjourned.]

APPENDIX

Material Submitted for the Record

SUBCOMMITTEE HEARING NOTICE
COMMITTEE ON FOREIGN AFFAIRS
U.S. HOUSE OF REPRESENTATIVES
WASHINGTON, DC 20515-6128

Subcommittee on Africa, Global Health, Global Human Rights, and International Organizations
Christopher H. Smith (R-NJ), Chairman

July 9, 2015

TO: MEMBERS OF THE COMMITTEE ON FOREIGN AFFAIRS

You are respectfully requested to attend an OPEN hearing of the Committee on Foreign Affairs, to be held by the Subcommittee on Africa, Global Health, Global Human Rights, and International Organizations in Room 2200 of the Rayburn House Office Building (and available live on the Committee website at http://www.ForeignAffairs.house.gov):

DATE: Thursday, July 9, 2015

TIME: 2:00 p.m.

SUBJECT: Africa's Displaced People

WITNESSES: Panel I
Ms. Catherine Wiesner
Deputy Assistant Secretary of State
Bureau of Population, Refugees, and Migration
U.S. Department of State

Mr. Thomas H. Staal
Acting Assistant Administrator
Bureau for Democracy, Conflict, and Humanitarian Assistance
U.S. Agency for International Development

Panel II
Mr. John Stauffer
President
The America Team for Displaced Eritreans

Ms. Ann Hollingsworth
Senior Advocate for Government Relations
Refugees International

Ms. Natalie Eisenbarth
Policy & Advocacy Officer
International Rescue Committee

By Direction of the Chairman

The Committee on Foreign Affairs seeks to make its facilities accessible to persons with disabilities. If you are in need of special accommodations, please call 202/225-5021 at least four business days in advance of the event, whenever practicable. Questions with regard to special accommodations in general (including availability of Committee materials in alternative formats and assistive listening devices) may be directed to the Committee.

COMMITTEE ON FOREIGN AFFAIRS

MINUTES OF SUBCOMMITTEE ON _Africa, Global Health, Global Human Rights, and International Organizations_ HEARING

Day__ _Thursday_ __Date_____ _July 9, 2015_ ____Room_ _2200 Rayburn HOB_

Starting Time __ _2:08 p.m._ ___Ending Time __ _4:30 p.m._

Recesses |_0_| (____to ____) (____to ____) (____to ____) (____to ____) (____to ____) (____to ____)

Presiding Member(s)

Rep. Chris Smith, Rep. Mark Meadows

Check all of the following that apply:

Open Session ☑   Electronically Recorded (taped) ☑
Executive (closed) Session ☐   Stenographic Record ☑
Televised ☑

TITLE OF HEARING:

Africa's Displaced People

SUBCOMMITTEE MEMBERS PRESENT:

Rep. Curt Clawson, Rep. David Cicilline, Rep. Karen Bass

NON-SUBCOMMITTEE MEMBERS PRESENT: _(Mark with an * if they are not members of full committee.)_

HEARING WITNESSES: Same as meeting notice attached? Yes ☑ No ☐
(If "no", please list below and include title, agency, department, or organization.)

STATEMENTS FOR THE RECORD: _(List any statements submitted for the record.)_

Full opening statement of Rep. Chris Smith, submitted for the record by Rep. Chris Smith
Refugees International Field Report, submitted for the record by Ms. Ann Hollingsworth
Report on Integrated Community Case Management at the International Rescue Committee, submitted for
the record by Ms. Natalie Eisenbarth
Statement of the U.S. Committee for Refugees and Immigrants, submitted for the record by Rep. Chris Smith

TIME SCHEDULED TO RECONVENE _____
or
TIME ADJOURNED __ _4:30 p.m._

Gregory B. Simpkins
Subcommittee Staff Director

"Africa's Displaced People"

Statement of Rep. Chris Smith
Subcommittee on Africa, Global Health, Global Human Rights and International Organizations
July 9, 2015

Last year, nearly 60 million people were displaced worldwide. In fact, one out of every 122 people on Earth today is either a refugee, internally displaced in their home country or seeking asylum in another country.

In sub-Saharan Africa, there are more than 15 million displaced people. Of that total, 3.7 million are refugees and 11.4 million are internally displaced. These disruptions of normal life in Africa are caused by conflicts such as in Somalia, the Central African Republic, South Sudan, Nigeria, the Democratic Republic of Congo, Mali, Burundi, Western Sahara and elsewhere. These disruptions not only affect those who are displaced, but also the people in whose communities these displaced people are relocated.

African refugees and internally displaced people face numerous issues - from security in the places in which they seek refuge, to death and mayhem trying to reach places of refuge, to conflict with surrounding populations to warehousing that consigns generations to be born and live in foreign countries.

Today's hearing will examine the various issues displaced people face and the U.S. response to these conditions in order to determine the effectiveness of our government's efforts to help and to determine whether course corrections are necessary.

The terrible plight of African refugees has been much in the news in recent months because of the death of thousands trying to reach Europe across the Mediterranean Sea and attacks on refugees in South Africa reportedly caused by xenophobia.

On the South African case, I sent two members of my staff to southern Africa last month to look into the incidents of violence against refugees in South Africa. What they found was appalling. Despite a very generous set of laws and programs to enable immigration into South Africa, refugees were often refused medical service at hospitals that supposedly offer free medical care to all people.

Apparently, no matter what the law in South Africa says, staff who screen patients often simply refuse to allow people they consider foreigners to receive medical care. According to refugees who spoke with my staff, this has meant that refugee women have had to give birth on the floor of hospitals while hospital staff refused to provide services.

As for those refugees trying to cross the Mediterranean to seek sanctuary in Europe, more than 1,800 people have died making that trip this year as of early June. On the cover of the April 25th issue of *The Economist* magazine, the failure of the nations of Europe to devise a workable, humane policy toward those fleeing to their continent was described as "a moral and political disgrace."

Many of the refugees trying to cross the Mediterranean are Eritreans, who also have fled persecution and repression at home through the Gulf of Aden and also through the Sinai

Peninsula, where they are often at the mercy of ruthless Bedouin groups, who traffic them or hold them for ransom. Eritrea is a closed society, so our knowledge of conditions there comes mostly from refugees, but one has to ask how bad must conditions there be if so many Eritreans are willing to risk their lives and well-being to find refugee almost anywhere else?

Unresolved conflicts have forced many refugees to experience protracted stays in foreign countries. For example, refugees have not only had children but also grandchildren in camps in Kenya and Algeria. After more than two decades, the situation in Somalia remains unresolved, and Somali refugees are unable to resume their lives in their homeland. Yet they face an increasingly hostile Kenyan environment in which the government is unwilling to allow Somalis to establish financial independence outside refugee camps.

In Algeria, Sahrawis, refugees from the Western Sahara territory under the control of Morocco, have lived in camps in western Algeria since being chased out of the territory by the advance of hundreds of thousands of Moroccans in 1975. The Government of Algeria not only provides a home for the Sahrawis, but also supplies access to free education and health care. Still, income-generating activities by Sahrawis are discouraged to prevent competition with local Algerians.

Internally displaced persons also face serious challenges. In Nigeria, for example, more than 1.5 million people from northeastern Nigeria have fled attacks by Boko Haram and resulting Nigerian military activities. However, Nigeria is a patchwork of 36 states whose creation over the years has inflamed ethnic and religious tensions as state majorities became minorities suddenly. The Nigerian IDPs are generally living in communities rather than camps. The longer they remain in their current areas, the greater the chance their presence will inflame new unrest as the ethnic and religious balance in their new areas is again changed abruptly.

The United States and the rest of the international community face serious challenges in addressing the displacement of so many people. According to U.N. High Commissioner for Refugees Antonio Guterres, the "international response capacities are overstretched by the unprecedented rise in global forced displacement." We must carefully consider the U.S. role in meeting the increasing challenge of Africa's displaced people, taking into consideration our moral imperative to help those in need, as well as strategic interests in preventing the kind of neglect that makes terrorist recruitment among displaced people easier than it should be.

MATERIAL SUBMITTED FOR THE RECORD BY MS. ANN HOLLINGSWORTH, SENIOR
ADVOCATE FOR GOVERNMENT RELATIONS, REFUGEES INTERNATIONAL

Refugees International Field Report
July 9, 2015
Sudanese Refugees in Chad: Passing the Baton to No One
Authors: Michael Boyce and Ann Hollingsworth

More than ten years after first arriving in Chad, over 360,000 Sudanese refugees are now dealing with a new reality. In the face of dramatic food ration cuts, and after years of shrinking support from the international community, aid agencies are pushing these refugees to become self-sufficient and more deeply integrated with their Chadian hosts. With the global humanitarian system overstretched, a more sustainable and targeted assistance strategy for this population would seem reasonable. But the early stages of this transition have encountered serious problems. These ration cuts, now in place for 18 months, have been devastating for already vulnerable households. Humanitarian funding has dried up and not been replaced by desperately-needed development activities. It is unrealistic to expect refugees to become self-sufficient in a place where livelihood opportunities are hard to find, government services are limited, cost of living is high, host community tensions are increasing, and most crucially, little development funding exists. It is time for the international community to recommit itself to this long-suffering population, and to do so in a sustainable way.

Policy Recommendations:

- Donors and the World Food Program (WFP) must immediately increase food rations to 2,100 kilocalories per day for vulnerable Sudanese refugees, until such time as assistance can be adjusted in line with a region-wide household economic assessment.
- The UN Refugee Agency (UNHCR) and the WFP should closely monitor the food security situation of Sudanese refugees after food assistance is adjusted. After 12 months, UNHCR and WFP should commission a full Joint Impact Evaluation to identify any necessary adjustments and to more fully understand and address coping mechanisms.
- Donors – especially the United States Agency for International Development, the German Federal Ministry for Economic Cooperation and Development, the Swiss Agency for Development and Cooperation, the European Union's Directorate-General for International Cooperation and Development, and the World Bank – should provide dedicated funding for development and resilience initiatives in eastern Chad that benefit both Sudanese refugees and Chadian host communities. Donors should also work with the Chadian government to make sure these populations are prioritized in the country's National Development Plan.
- The UN Development Program, the Food and Agriculture Organization, the UN Children's Education Fund, and the UN Population Fund should deploy additional program staff to eastern Chad in accordance with their respective responsibilities under the UN Integrated Strategy for the Sahel, and should work with the UNHCR to implement development and resilience initiatives on the basis of need.
- In refugee-hosting areas, donors and development agencies should prioritize efforts to improve water management, agricultural inputs and techniques, land management and dispute resolution, and women's empowerment.
- The UNHCR should freeze its budget for core refugee protection and assistance in eastern Chad. Further cuts should only be considered once refugees begin receiving long-term support from development actors.
- The Chadian government should strengthen healthcare services in refugee-hosting areas. In particular, the government should accelerate the hiring process for healthcare workers with foreign qualifications and pay incentives to healthcare workers who accept postings in underserved areas.
- The Chadian government must pay for all necessary salaries and equipment for the Detachment for the Protection of Humanitarians and Refugees.

Background:

Though its most recent civil war ended in 2009, Chad shares more than half of its borders with conflict-affected countries: Nigeria, the Central African Republic, Sudan, and Libya. After years of conflict between the Chadian

President Idriss Déby and Sudanese President Omar al-Bashir, the two reached a rapprochement in 2010 that stabilized the country's eastern border. Yet regional counterterrorism efforts, particularly with respect to Boko Haram, remain a primary focus of the Chadian government. The June 15, 2015 suicide bombings in the Chadian capital N'Djamena, which targeted both the police academy and the police headquarters, have heightened security protocols in and around the city.

In addition to these security concerns, Chad faces both long-term development challenges and recent, acute economic concerns. Chad ranks 184th out of 187 countries in the UN's Human Development Index. Living conditions for both refugees and host communities alike are very difficult, with food insecurity and a lack of livelihood opportunities just a few of the challenges they face. The price of oil, the country's main export, has fallen roughly 40 percent since last year, and trade routes into Nigeria, Central African Republic, and Libya have been largely cut due to conflict. As a result, the World Bank reports that government spending on services and development will decline significantly in 2015, and could fall even further if Chad's military campaign against Boko Haram expands.

At a time when the international community is shifting its focus to new refugee flows from both the Central African Republic and Nigeria, Chad's Sudanese refugee population has struggled to stay on the radar. The Sudanese refugees' exile has become protracted, and their chances of achieving durable solutions are low. Permanent return to Sudan is unlikely, as the security situation inside Darfur remains extremely volatile and internal displacement has risen to levels not seen since 2004. Resettlement of Sudanese refugees remains limited to the most vulnerable cases, despite appeals for broader, group resettlement. Local integration, meanwhile, has not proved attractive for many refugees, and RI was told that bureaucratic roadblocks also prevent interested refugees from gaining Chadian citizenship. In the meantime, the extremely large numbers of refugees – as much as half the total population of some Chadian departments – continues to put great strain on services and natural resources.

Despite appearances of being an unchanged population, the number of Sudanese refugees in Chad continues to increase. According to the UN Refugee Agency (UNHCR), roughly 70,000 Sudanese have been born in exile and 36,000 new refugees arrived in 2013. The shifting conflict in Darfur, and the possible withdrawal or drawdown of the UN-African Union Mission in Darfur (UNAMID), could eventually lead to increased refugee flows into Chad. Indeed, during a May 2015 mission to the country, a Refugees International team met one refugee who had arrived in Chad just one week prior, having never been displaced before.

Food Ration Cuts: Fixing the Mistake, Finding a Way Forward

In early 2014, the World Food Program (WFP) made a dramatic 50 percent cut (up to 60 percent in some areas) in food rations for Sudanese refugees in Chad: from the previous allotment of 2,100 kilocalories a day to around 800.

RI saw first-hand the effect of these cuts at a food distribution inside Am Nabak refugee camp. In addition to reductions in legumes, sorghum, oil, and cereals, no sugar or salt were available to the refugees. Soap happened to be part of the distribution that day but that had not been included in months, according to the refugees.

While there were some attempts to warn the refugees of the impending cuts, the refugees that RI spoke with were clearly still in disbelief about this change, and they explained that access to food remains a key challenge in their daily lives. After the ration cuts began, one humanitarian worker said that the most vulnerable in the refugee camps had to begin "begging to their neighbors."

In Touloum refugee camp, RI spoke with two female refugees in their 30s who said it was difficult to get their children the necessary nutrition, particularly since the food rations began, as local food is expensive and items such as fruit or meat are not provided by WFP. Humanitarians that RI spoke with said women often cannot afford essentials such as milk for their children. One local NGO spoke to RI about malnourished children having to share their nutritional supplements with their families since the ration cuts began, prolonging their recovery time.

Even households who are manifestly unable to support themselves have not been spared the cuts. RI spoke with Kaltuma, whose husband was killed in Darfur. Her mother is too weak to work so she must care for her, along with three orphans she has taken into her home. She said she had no way to support them and was worried about her future.

Both refugees and aid workers told RI that refugees – particularly women and children – had responded to the cuts with worrying coping mechanisms. Women RI spoke with left camps to find what little work they could, often farming or making bricks. Sometimes these trips would last for days or weeks at a time, with children being taken out of school either to work or care for younger siblings while their parents were gone. An operational NGO worker that RI spoke with noted an increase in cases of sexual violence and exploitation against the Sudanese refugee women since the ration cuts began. Petty crime has increased in some areas as well.

These ration cuts occurred at a time when the Sudanese refugee population was also dealing with major cuts to other longstanding support – including for non-food items and firewood. Aid officials told RI that the refugees had long worked to build up their savings and to buy household items. But they noted that since the ration cuts, refugees had to work in order to eat, regardless of how vulnerable they might be or what kinds of services (such as education or healthcare) they might forgo in order to earn money.

In 2014, UNCHR conducted a nutrition survey to look at the impact on the population after the food ration cuts occurred. Though at least three camps showed Global Acute Malnutrition rates at critical levels (above 15 percent), the results indicated that malnutrition rates for the entire refugee population had decreased slightly since 2013. This assessment was not entirely shared by some aid workers RI spoke with, who said they had seen a modest rise in malnutrition cases presented at health clinics. Refugees, too, disputed this claim, telling RI that malnutrition had increased in some camps and that children were often sick for months at a time. "When mothers aren't well, children also suffer," one female refugee told RI. "Our sisters and mothers look in the mirror and in their own eyes, they see the effect of the ration cuts."

Despite the survey results, it was clear to RI that the consequences of food ration cuts for the most vulnerable households have been unacceptable. A short-term increase in food assistance for those households is absolutely essential. Therefore, donors and the WFP must immediately increase food rations to the 2,100 kilocalories per day for vulnerable Sudanese refugees.

WFP and UNHCR are in the process of executing a new approach to food assistance for the Sudanese refugees – one in which aid is targeted on the basis of need. The two agencies are conducting economic assessments that will divide households into four groups, from very poor to better off. Full rations would only be provided for poorer households – roughly 60 percent of all refugees, according to preliminary data. Wealthier households would receive more limited amounts of food or non-food assistance (such as food-for-assets and access to microcredit) according to their means. UN officials project that the transition to this new approach will be completed by the end of 2015.

Aid officials admit that this change was driven, in part, by a lack of funding. "We have to shift to a vulnerability-based approach to assistance instead of a rights-based approach," one said. "We don't have the resources to do the latter." If well executed, this vulnerability-based approach could give some refugees greater economic opportunity, as well as more freedom to purchase the kinds of food that they prefer. However, some officials whom RI spoke to feared that donors were reluctant to fund certain parts of the plan – particularly the assistance for middle-income or wealthier households. They expressed concern that if the most vulnerable refugees were the only ones receiving aid, or if the population experienced a shock like drought, more households could become impoverished due to neglect.

To ensure that this new approach to food aid is successful, UNHCR and WFP should closely monitor the food security situation of Sudanese refugees after assistance is adjusted in line with region-wide household economic assessments. After 12 months, UNHCR and WFP should commission a full Joint Impact Evaluation to identify any necessary adjustments and to more fully understand and address coping mechanisms.

A Haphazard Shift to Self-Reliance

For most of their 12 years in exile, the Sudanese refugees in Chad were treated by donors and aid agencies as a purely humanitarian concern. UNHCR, WFP, and other organizations provided the kinds of direct assistance that any refugee population might expect: food rations, shelter, non-food items, water, healthcare, education, and protection. Seemingly little thought was given to the sustainability of this aid, or to ways of making the refugees more self-sufficient. During RI's visits to four Sudanese refugee camps in eastern Chad, the physical evidence of this was plain to see: camp schools, not built for the long-term, are now in disrepair; gas-powered generators brought in to power water pumps are now breaking down. Just as disconcerting is what humanitarians see as the population's dependence on aid. With limited livelihood opportunities available in eastern Chad, and few attempts by aid agencies to create new ones, refugees naturally grew to rely on emergency assistance. This was reflected in RI's discussions with refugees about the ration cuts discussed above: when asked what could be done to address the problem, a typical response from a refugee would be, "You need to make things the way they were before."

In the last two years, however, the humanitarian community in eastern Chad has begun to move toward a self-reliance approach for the Sudanese refugees. This self-reliance approach has four main pillars:

1. Pursuing an "Alternatives to Camps" policy by providing assistance to refugees who choose to settle in nearby communities, and carrying out quick impact projects in support of those communities.
2. Pursuing socio-economic "solutions" for the refugees, including land access for refugees and broader support for agriculture in refugee-hosting areas.
3. Replacing the Sudanese curriculum with the Chadian curriculum in refugee primary and secondary schools, and bringing refugee schools under the oversight of the Chadian Ministry of Education.
4. Integrating health services for refugees into the Chadian national health system and requiring wealthier refugee households to pay for healthcare.

In principle, this transition is laudable. It follows years of research suggesting that displaced people lead more dignified lives if they are self-sufficient and integrated with host communities. However, in eastern Chad this transition faces a major – and potentially fatal – obstacle: the communities that refugees are meant to join are some of the poorest in the world, with extremely weak institutions, markets, and social services. In the words of one humanitarian whom RI spoke to, "Everybody is talking about socio-economic integration…but how do you integrate refugees into an area where people are starving?"

Of the roughly 360,000 Sudanese refugees resident in Chad, about 75 percent live in the Sahel, the eco-climactic zone just south of the Sahara Desert. As described by the UN, the Sahel's 100 million residents face "recurring food and nutritional crises caused by climate change, environmental degradation, drought, floods, poorly functioning markets, low agricultural productivity, poverty and conflict [which] have seriously eroded the ability of households to withstand repeated and increasingly frequent shocks." The region is also exceptionally vulnerable to climate change, with a temperature rise of between 7 and 10 degrees Fahrenheit expected by mid-century.

The comprehensive humanitarian assistance given to the Sudanese refugees has insulated them from these harsh conditions, but their Chadian neighbors have not been so fortunate. According to one official RI spoke with, 15 of Chad's 32 Sahelian departments currently face emergency-level rates of global acute malnutrition, with rates as high as 21 percent in some refugee-hosting areas. Agricultural production is seriously insufficient due to poor soil quality (aggravated by progressive deforestation), limited use of modern farming techniques, and rapid population growth. Water shortages are chronic, with host communities often having less access to potable water than the refugees. Both refugees and Chadian villagers told RI that they frequently had to collect untreated water from seasonal rivers, where water-borne diseases are common.

Though these problems have been obvious for years, the Chadian government and foreign donors have failed to address them in a comprehensive, sustainable way. President Déby has won praise abroad for establishing stability and growing the economy, but aid agencies point out that poor Chadians – in the Sahel zone and elsewhere – have been left behind. According to the UN, more than 80 percent of health clinics in the country are "non-functional" or lack the necessary equipment and personnel, with the eastern regions especially underserved. More than 75 percent of teachers receive no compensation from government sources, and RI was told that in the Sahel, many children are only able to attend school because of WFP-supplied school meals. One father living in the eastern village of Foyou, not far from Treguine refugee camp, told RI that his children attend school "under the tree."

In such a difficult context, integrating refugees with their host communities without providing substantial aid to both groups will not lead to self-reliance. The UNHCR, WFP, and their humanitarian partners can provide a safety net for the most vulnerable, but eastern Chad's chronic problems actually require development solutions. RI was therefore dismayed by the severe weakness of the UN's development agencies in eastern Chad, and particularly the Sahelian regions thereof. Of these agencies, the most troubling were the United Nations Development Program (UNDP), whose two small offices in the east have recently been downsized, forcing the agency to shut down key projects intended to serve refugees and locals alike; and the Food and Agriculture Organization (FAO), which recently closed its only office in the east due to lack of funding. One senior humanitarian RI spoke with described UNDP's feebleness in the region as "a great source of frustration."

The lack of development actors and activities in eastern Chad has already critically undermined efforts by the UN Resident Coordinator/Humanitarian Coordinator (RC/HC) and humanitarian agencies to build resilience in the east – for refugees and their hosts alike. In the Sila region, for example, the RC/HC and the regional governor approved a four-year regional resilience strategy in June 2013 that was intended to address the needs of both refugees and local residents. UNDP was charged with leading or supporting 19 of the strategy's 37 tasks, but the UNDP staffer dedicated to implementing the strategy was withdrawn in early 2015.

In the absence of development actors, UNHCR and its NGO partners have attempted to fill the gap with their own resilience and development programs in refugee-hosting areas. In doing so they have received commendable (if limited) support from the U.S. Department of State's Bureau for Population, Refugees, and Migration; and GIZ, the German development corporation. However, UNHCR cannot and should not lead the UN's development response in the east. The organization's humanitarian focus, lack of technical expertise for development, and its year-to-year budget cycle make it unsuitable for development activities. This has been proven during decades of failed attempts by UNHCR to create development solutions for refugee populations on its own. Moreover, other UN agencies have the necessary mandates and capabilities to carry out this work in eastern Chad. The UN Security Council itself acknowledged this when it endorsed the UN Integrated Strategy for the Sahel in July 2013 – a strategy that established specific responsibilities for each UN agency working in the region. Confusing these responsibilities in Chad would set an unhelpful precedent for the UN system both in the Sahel and worldwide.

Humanitarian officials in Chad whom RI spoke to – including donors, UN officials, and international and local NGOs – were unanimous in their demand for greater involvement in the east by development donors and agencies. Even one development official admitted to RI that "the transition from relief to development in the east has failed."

RI therefore believes that in line with their respective responsibilities under the UN Integrated Strategy for the Sahel, UNDP, FAO, the UN Children's Education Fund (UNICEF), and the UN Population Fund (UNFPA) should deploy additional program staff to eastern Chad, and should work with UNHCR to implement development and resilience initiatives on the basis of need. Since these agencies have so far not prioritized eastern Chad within their country strategies, RI also believes that donors who have already expressed some interest in the region – especially the United States Agency for International Development, the German Federal Ministry for Economic Cooperation and Development, the Swiss Agency for Development and Cooperation, the European Union's Directorate-General for International Cooperation and Development, and the World Bank – must provide dedicated funding for development and resilience initiatives in eastern Chad that benefit both Sudanese refugees and Chadian host communities.

This report does not endeavor to present a full-fledged development and resilience strategy for eastern Chad; indeed, a national resilience strategy for Chad is already being drafted under the auspices of the Global Alliance for Resilience (also known as AGIR). In addition, there are existing guidebooks for resilience programming that could help donors and aid agencies plan their responses. However, RI's numerous interviews with aid officials, refugees, and Chadians did uncover a few priority interventions that donors and aid agencies should consider: water management, agricultural inputs and techniques, dispute resolution, and women's empowerment.

Particularly in eastern Chad's Sahelian zone, access to water is a major challenge. Groundwater collection is difficult, with existing wells built by humanitarians requiring regular and costly maintenance. Seasonal rainwater flows out of the region quickly, with not enough captured for use during the lengthy dry season. The resulting water shortages have impacts well beyond the lack of water for household use: the amount of arable land, and the ability of families to farm year-round, is limited; and the constant search for distant water sources puts women and children at risk. Sudanese refugees living in the region also told RI that eastern Chad's water problems were unlike those they had faced in Darfur, so the population has a clear need for water management training, tools, and infrastructure.

Agriculture was an economic mainstay for most Sudanese refugees before they went into exile, and it has remained their primary livelihood in Chad. During the planting and harvest seasons, it is typical for more than half of the refugees to leave their camps in search of farm work, often for months at a stretch. However, both the refugees and their hosts face a scarcity of arable land. Refugees told RI that in return for land access, they typically must pay Chadian landowners either half of their harvest or the equivalent in cash. This has been a major source of frustration for the refugees. "We hosted these people back when they were refugees in Sudan, and we did not treat them this way," one refugee told RI. Yet their Chadian hosts are also under pressure. "The refugee camp sits on land that we used to farm," one villager living near Treguine camp said. "We also have to share pasture land with the refugees, so many of our cattle have died from hunger."

To enable both refugees and their hosts to earn a living from the land – and to continue doing so as temperatures and rainfall shift due to climate change – efforts should be made to both increase the amount of arable land (potentially through the use of irrigation or soil rehabilitation) and increase its productivity through improved farming inputs and techniques.

A related and critical area of concern is dispute resolution between refugees, their Chadian neighbors, and local authorities. Though many of the refugees and locals share an ethnicity and language, resource scarcity has pushed them into conflict. For example, refugee women told RI that they often face abuse when collecting firewood or farming outside their camps. "People say, 'You're a refugee! What are you doing here?'" one said. "Women can be raped, and then they are so ashamed that they do not report it." Refugees also complained that nomadic herders graze animals on the land they were farming, often leading to violence between the two groups.

Both refugees and Chadians spoke approvingly of "mixed committees" formed at the initiative of UNHCR and its NGO partners, where elders from both communities gather to address disputes. But they added that certain problems (such as the demarcation of land for farmers and herders) remained unresolved and required further discussion and help from aid agencies. In addition, one humanitarian familiar with the mixed committees told RI that donor support for the project was being cut, despite a need for more engagement. Land disputes in the resource-limited Sahel are commonplace, and have previously contributed to devastating, broader conflicts – including in Darfur itself. Therefore the need for dispute resolution and peaceful coexistence in eastern Chad should be obvious. Donor support for dispute resolution should increase, with Chadian authorities providing support as needed.

A final, overarching priority for development donors and agencies must be women's empowerment. Sudanese refugee women and girls suffer from a low social status, with limited rights and economic power. This contributes to gender-based violence (including rape, domestic violence, and early or forced marriage), poor maternal health, high fertility rates, and the vulnerability of women-headed households. Any long-term strategy for eastern Chad must address the consequences and causes of women's disempowerment. For example, the recent decree by President Déby fixing 18 as the legal age of marriage in Chad provides an important opening for programs that promote girls' social rights, girls' education, and sexual and reproductive health.

Unfortunately, it is hard to imagine that eastern Chad's development challenges will be addressed quickly, so it is essential that humanitarian assistance continue for both refugees and host communities. In this regard, RI is deeply concerned about repeated, deep cuts to UNHCR's budget for eastern Chad. Refugees, NGOs, and Chadian authorities whom RI spoke with universally echoed one observer's frustration: "The needs here are still high, and even increasing. How can UNHCR possibly keep cutting?"

Already, UNHCR's cuts have encouraged – if not forced – various international implementing partners to leave eastern Chad. Those who remain have seen their grants from UNHCR reduced by as much as 40 percent in the last two years. International NGOs still working in the east told RI they could not meet UNHCR's programmatic expectations with the funding it provides. Local NGOs, whose role has grown significantly in recent years, are almost exclusively funded by UNHCR in the areas that RI visited in eastern Chad.

UNHCR's budget is, of course, under enormous strain globally. Yet, as this report has made clear, UNHCR cannot step back from eastern Chad if development actors do not step forward. The UNHCR should not make further cuts to its budget for core refugee protection and assistance in eastern Chad. Further cuts should only be considered once refugees begin receiving long-term support from development actors, and even then UNHCR support to the most vulnerable must continue.

Chad's Challenges and Opportunities

The Chadian government has welcomed Sudanese refugees onto its territory for more than a decade, and it has allowed humanitarians to operate in the east without serious interference. But what the government has not done is make significant investments toward developing the east. Until now, this has not had a major impact on the lives of the Sudanese refugees, since their needs have been addressed by humanitarians. But it has affected their Chadian neighbors, who receive substantially less international assistance and are, as a result, often more vulnerable than the refugees.

As noted above, any effort to make the Sudanese refugees self-reliant, or to integrate them with their Chadian hosts, will have to address this glaring gap. And it will require the Chadian government to provide policy direction and funding. Three priority areas for government action emerged from RI's research in the east: development planning, healthcare, and security.

First, the government should prioritize the east – and especially refugee-hosting areas – in its National Development Plan, and ensure that this is further reinforced at the regional and local levels. It should also endorse the specific development and resilience activities outlined above. Together, these measures would give development agencies and donors a clear mandate to intervene on behalf of Sudanese refugees and their hosts.

Second, the Chadian government must strengthen healthcare services in refugee-hosting areas. As part of its self-reliance strategy, the UNHCR and the Chadian authorities decided that Sudanese refugees would no longer receive healthcare at separate facilities, but would instead be served through the Chadian national health system. Though a fine idea in principle, in fact health services in the east's refugee-hosting regions have been critically weakened by a lack of state healthcare workers. Aid agencies told RI that in many parts of the east, Chadian state clinics are almost entirely staffed by NGO workers paid by UNHCR and its partners. These aid agencies claim that many state-funded healthcare posts at these clinics remain vacant. They also note that when state healthcare workers are deployed, many quit because their salaries are too low or, in some cases, not paid at all. One aid worker went so far as to say that without UNHCR and its implementing partners, many state clinics in eastern Chad would be defunct.

The Chadian government can address these problems in two relatively modest ways. First, the government should create – and implement – a system of financial incentives for healthcare workers who accept postings in underserved areas. This would be particularly helpful in the refugee-hosting eastern regions, where the cost of living is high and living conditions are difficult compared with other parts of Chad. In addition, the government should accelerate its hiring process for healthcare workers with foreign qualifications. RI was told by one aid agency that the accreditation of foreign-trained healthcare workers by the Chadian Ministry of Health had stalled, creating a large backlog of potentially qualified doctors and nurses. The government should work through this backlog without delay.

Third and finally, the Chadian government must demonstrate that it is serious about creating a secure operating environment for humanitarians, development actors, and the people they serve. Due to banditry and other security concerns in eastern Chad, UN staffers are not permitted to travel beyond the region's main towns without an armed escort. And since July 2013, a gendarme division, the Detachment for the Protection of Humanitarians and Refugees (DPHR), has been charged with providing that service. Yet numerous humanitarian and security officials told RI that despite repeated requests, the government has failed to provide the DPHR with the equipment and salaries it needs to operate. As a consequence, UN agencies are forced to pay and equip the DPHR if they want to reach their beneficiaries. In the words of one official RI spoke to, "The government knows that humanitarians will pay in the end, so then they don't have to."

Clearly, this arrangement will not bring lasting security to the east, nor will it encourage development donors and agencies to direct their scarce resources to this region. The Chadian government must therefore shoulder its responsibility and pay for all necessary salaries and equipment for the DPHR. It should also ensure that DPHR personnel are made available to aid agencies irrespective of whether they are assisting host communities or refugees, and whether or not those agencies are humanitarians.

Conclusion:

How to best assist a long-term refugee population such as the Sudanese refugees in eastern Chad is not a new problem. Development and self-reliance initiatives, combined with a strong safety net for the most vulnerable, appear to be the best options in the absence of durable solutions. But without the necessary funding and leadership, this population's suffering will only increase. The Sudanese refugees deserve more than an empty promise, and the international community must refocus its efforts to meet this challenge.

Michael Boyce and Ann Hollingsworth visited Chad in May and June 2015. They met with refugees, host communities, humanitarians, development actors, and government officials in the regions of N'Djamena, Wadi Fira, and Ouaddaï.

MATERIAL SUBMITTED FOR THE RECORD BY MS. NATALIE EISENBARTH, POLICY &
ADVOCACY OFFICER, INTERNATIONAL RESCUE COMMITTEE

Impact, Utilization and Quality of Integrated Community Case Management at The International
Rescue Committee

Reach of IRC's Integrated Community Case Management Programming
Global

The IRC covers a population of more than 3.5 million children across six countries and 17
districts, through a network of more than 12,000 community health workers. Over a decade, the
IRC's integrated community case management programs have provided more than 4.8 million
treatments to children under the age of five for malaria, pneumonia and diarrhea.

The findings from the different methods used to monitor project performance converge to
highlight that, overall, the project has been a continuous source of effective drugs to treat the
main killers of children in many rural areas where other sources of effective drugs are scarce.

Community demand for CHWs' services has been good for fever and suspected pneumonia and
unsatisfactory for diarrhea. The CHWs have enough skills to provide correct treatment for the
child's main complaint and to refer children with danger signs. Unfortunately, many CHWs still
fail to identify conditions not reported by the mother, not to give antibiotics to children with
simple cough, and to manage conditions that require referral despite not being a danger sign.

Despite important, these cases do not constitute the majority of the CHWs' workload. A
conservative estimate suggests that the program may have provided appropriate treatment to one
third of the malaria cases and one fifth of the pneumonia cases. This is clearly an average for the
six countries; the final survey findings show that in some project areas the coverage was
extremely high. The program suggests a decrease in child mortality above 20%.

	Child U5 seen by Community Health Workers	Total treatment given by Community Health Workers
2004-2012	2,421,200	3,549,544
2013-2014	1,122,027	1,310,704
TOTAL 2004-2014	3,543,227	4,860,248

Impact on Child Mortality
Sierra Leone and South Sudan

IRC's impact in child mortality suggests that the program is associated to a 21.0% decrease in
mortality of children 2-59 months of age over a two-year period in Sierra Leone and a 26.4%
decrease in mortality among children under five over a five-year period in South Sudan. Despite
information on coverage and utilization converging to highlight the important role of the
Community Health Workers (CHWs) in access to treatment for the main killers of children under
five, in both cases it is unclear whether the decline is solely attributable to the integrated
community case management (iCCM) program.

Curative Coverage
Sierra Leone and South Sudan

The available information regarding coverage of curative interventions from the final household
surveys in Sierra Leone and South Sudan show high coverage of appropriate treatment of fever,

diarrhea and suspected pneumonia in both countries. Most of the sick children with malaria, diarrhea or pneumonia got appropriate treatment from community health workers (44.6% - 82.6%).

	Curative coverage data		
	Sierra Leone	Sierra Leone	South Sudan
Appropriate treatment for fever (ACT) *from CHW*	45.5%	58.2%	73.5%
Appropriate treatment for diarrhea (ORS + zinc) *from CHW*	28.9%	44.6%	82.6%
Appropriate treatment for suspected pneumonia (antibiotic for LRTI) *from CHW*		58.8%	75.3%
Source	Mid-term mortality survey Kono District	Final mortality survey Kono District	Final mortality survey Panyijar County
Period	October 2010	January 2013	May 2012

An estimate of the actual coverage for all the countries and for the whole project length using routine data and incidence estimates for malaria, diarrhea and pneumonia suggests that the intervention covered about 34%, 7% and 17% of the expected episodes of malaria, diarrhea and pneumonia respectively.

Utilization

Utilization information over the life of the project has varied enormously among countries. While, through CHWs, an under five child in the IRC's project area received on average 0.5 treatments per year in Rwanda, a similar child received 3.1 treatments per year in South Sudan, six times more. In terms of source of care, and compared with health facilities, CHWs provide the majority of the malaria, diarrhea and pneumonia treatments in all countries.

Quality of Care

During the project cycle, the IRC triangulated supervision data to get greater insight into the quality of care provided by CHWs through assessments conducted by staff and MOH officials with advanced technical skills.

The project systems to assure quality showed that most CHWs are able to classify a child correctly, refer a child with general danger signs, provide the correct treatment to a child according to the age and condition and provide counseling on the administration of the drugs at home. About half of the literate CHWs record the information about the case correctly and close to half of them give the first dose during the encounter. CHWs have more problems to conduct a thorough assessment, and to provide the caregiver the key messages about home management of the sick child. The difficulty that many CHWs experience to assess pneumonia has come across loud and clear throughout the project life. The IRC successfully tested an approach to increase the CHWs ability to manage pneumonia and is actively advocating globally for context-specific tools or devices to help low literacy CHWs identify pneumonia.

Multi-country results on CHWs' quality of care assessments

Skill	Ethiopia	Uganda	South Sudan	Sierra Leone		Total
Assessment	83%	3%	0%	4%		22%
Age	100%	100%	29%	82%		83%
3 conditions	84%	63%	8%	8%		48%
Length	100%	97%	63%	84%		87%
5 danger signs	96%	3%	4%	16%		28%
Referral	93%	82%	75%	59%		77%
Classification	97%	80%	69%	91%		85%
Treatment		25%	40%	56%		37%
1st dose		32%	40%	56%		41%
Correct treatment	81%	61%	60%	94%		72%
Counseling	50%	11%	7%	13%		19%
Drugs	50%	57%	33%	81%		56%
Home management	75%	21%	13%	13%		33%
Recording	65%	50%		29%		49%
Illiterate	5%	70%	100%	15%		46%

MATERIAL SUBMITTED FOR THE RECORD BY THE HONORABLE CHRISTOPHER H. SMITH, A REPRESENTATIVE IN CONGRESS FROM THE STATE OF NEW JERSEY, AND CHAIRMAN, SUBCOMMITTEE ON AFRICA, GLOBAL HEALTH, GLOBAL HUMAN RIGHTS, AND INTERNATIONAL ORGANIZATIONS

Statement for the Record of the U.S. Committee for Refugees and Immigrants
Submitted to the House Committee on Foreign Affairs Subcommittee on Africa, Global Health, Global
Human Rights, and International Organizations
Hearing on "Africa's Displaced People"
July 9, 2015

For over 100 years, the U.S. Committee for Refugees and Immigrants (USCRI) has helped shape history by protecting refugees, serving immigrants and upholding freedom. In 2004, the USCRI embarked on a worldwide campaign to end the warehousing of refugees and released the 2004 World Refugee Survey – Warehousing Issue. Warehousing is the practice of keeping refugees in protracted situations of restricted mobility, enforced idleness, and dependency – their lives on indefinite hold – in violation of their basic rights under the 1951 UN Refugee Convention.

The UNHCR reports that world-wide displacement is at its highest recorded levels with 59.5 million people forcibly displaced at the end of 2014. Meanwhile, the international community's reception towards refugees has deteriorated with fear, push back and denial of human rights. In June 2015, the year-long United Nations Commission of inquiry released a report, which said that "the international community" should protect tens of thousands of Eritreans who have fled or continue to try to flee their country, and promote safe channels for regular migration, particularly for those attempting to cross the Mediterranean. Approximately 5,000 Eritreans are fleeing their country each month, the commission said.

USCRI supports the Subcommittee's "examination of the extent of Africa's displaced persons problem and the options our government has to respond to the continent's crises and help alleviate the suffering of millions of people." We need to call upon ourselves and the international community to treat refugees as equals and give them their human rights, while they are refugees, to support themselves and live normal lives in dignity.

Thank you.